IN A MONASTERY LIBRARY

PRESERVING CODEX SINAITICUS AND THE GREEK WRITTEN HERITAGE

Scot McKendrick

THE BRITISH LIBRARY

ΠΟΥΣΗΣΕΙΣΤΟΜΝΗ
ΜΕΙΟΝΚΑΙΒΛΕΠΕΙ
ΤΟΝΛΙΘΟΝΗΡΜΕΝ
ΑΠΟΤΗΣΘΥΡΑΣΕΚΤ
ΜΝΗΜΙΟΥ·ΤΡΕΧΕΙ
ΚΑΙΕΡΧΕΤΑΙΠΡΟ
ΣΙΜΩΝΑΠΕΤΡΟΝ·
ΚΑΙΠΡΟΣΤΟΝΑΛ
ΜΑΘΗΤΗΝΟΝΕΦΙ
ΛΕΙΟΙΣΚΑΙΛΕΓΕΙ
ΤΟΙΣΗΡΑΝΤΟΝΚΝ
ΕΚΤΟΥΜΝΗΜΙΟΥ·ΚΑΙ
ΟΥΚΟΙΔΑΜΕΝΠΟΥ
ΕΘΗΚΑΝΑΥΤΟΝ·ΕΞΗΛ
ΘΕΝΟΥΝΟΠΕΤΡΟΣ
ΚΑΙΟΑΛΛΟΣΜΑΘΗ
ΤΗΣΚΑΙΕΤΡΕΧΟΝ
ΔΥΟΟΜΟΥ·ΠΡΟΣ
ΔΡΑΜΕΝΔΕΤΑΧΙΟΝ
ΤΟΥΠΕΤΡΟΥΚΑΙΗΛ
ΘΕΝΕΙΣΤΟΜΝΗΜΙ
ΠΡΩΤΟΣΚΑΙΠΑΡΑ
ΤΑΣΒΛΕΠΕΙΤΑΟΘΟ
ΝΙΑΚΕΙΜΕΝΑ·ΟΥΚΝ
ΤΟΣΟΥΔΑΡΙΟΝΟΗΝ
ΕΠΙΤΗΣΚΕΦΑΛΗ
ΑΥΤΟΥΟΥΜΕΤΑΤΩΝ
ΟΘΟΝΙΩΝΚΕΙΜ
ΑΛΛΑΧΩΡΙΣΕΝΤ
ΛΙΓΜΕΝΟΝΕΙΣΕΝΑ
ΤΟΠΟΝΤΟΤΕΟΥΝ
ΕΙΣΗΛΘΕΝΚΑΙΟΑΛ

ΩΡΕΙΑΓΓΕΛΟΥΣΚΑ
ΘΕΖΟΜΕΝΟΥΣΕΝ
ΛΕΥΚΟΙΣΕΝΑΠΡΟ
ΤΗΚΕΦΑΛΗ·ΚΑΙΕ
ΝΑΠΡΟΣΤΟΙΣΠΟ
ΟΠΟΥΕΚΕΙΤΟΤΟ
ΣΩΜΑΤΟΥΙΥΛΕΓΟ
ΣΙΝΑΥΤΗΕΚΕΙΝ
ΓΥΝΑΙΤΙΚΛΑΕΙΣ·
ΛΕΓΕΙΑΥΤΟΙΣΟΤΙ
ΡΑΝΤΟΝΚΝΜΟΥΚ
ΟΥΚΟΙΔΑΠΟΥΕΘΗ
ΚΑΝΑΥΤΟΝ·
ΤΑΥΤΑΕΙΠΟΥΣΑΕΣΤΡΑ
ΦΗΕΙΣΤΑΟΠΙΣΩΚ
ΘΕΩΡΕΙΤΟΝΙΝ
ΕΣΤΩΤΑΚΑΙΟΥΚΗΔ
ΟΤΙΙΣΕΣΤΙΝ·ΛΕΓΕΙ
ΑΥΤΗΙΣΓΥΝΑΙΤΙ
ΚΛΑΙΕΙΣΤΙΝΑΖΗ
ΤΕΙΣΕΚΕΙΝΗΔΕ
ΚΟΥΣΑΟΤΙΟΚΗΠ
ΡΟΣΕΣΤΙΝΛΕΓΕΙΑΥ
ΤΩΚΕΕΙΣΥΕΒΑΣ
ΕΣΤΑΣΑΣΑΥΤΟΝ·ΕΙ
ΠΕΜΟΙΠΟΥΕΘΗ
ΚΑΣΑΥΤΟΝΚΑΓΩ
ΤΟΝΑΡΩ
ΛΕΓΕΙΑΥΤΗΟΙΣΜΑΡΙ
ΑΜ·ΣΤΡΑΦΕΙΣΑΔ
ΚΕΙΝΗΛΕΓΕΙΑΥΤ
ΡΑΒΒΟΥΝΕΙ

ΙΣΗΡΧΟΝΤΟΕΙΣΤΟ
ΜΝΗΜΙΟΝ

ΟΥΜΕΝΤΟΙΣΓΕΙΣΗΛΘΕΝ
ΕΡΧΕΤΑΙΟΥΝΚΑΙΣΙΜΩ
ΠΕΤΡΟΣΑΚΟΛΟΥΘΩΝ
ΑΥΤΩΤΩΝΕΙΣΗΛΘΕΝΕΙΣ
ΤΟΜΝΗΜΕΙΟΝΚΑΙΘΕΩ
ΡΙΤΑΟΘΟΝΙΑΚΕΙΜΕΝΑ

PRESERVING CODEX SINAITICUS

Codex Sinaiticus is a treasure beyond price. Often described in super-latives, this ancient handwritten book is hard to overestimate for its deep and continuing significance. For many scholars it is the pre-eminent Christian Bible, known to them as 'Aleph' or 'number one'. Amongst Christians worldwide it is renowned for containing the earliest complete copy of the New Testament. Arguably it is also the earliest Christian Bible, the ultimate antecedent of all printed editions of the Bible in what-ever language. As one of the earliest luxury *codices*, or bound books, to survive in large part, the Codex forms one of the most important land-marks in the history of the book. What is more, its pages offer some of the most direct links with a crucial turning point in world history, the triumph of the Emperor Constantine the Great at the Battle of the Milvian Bridge in AD 312 and the Edict of Milan of AD 313 in which Constantine formally recognised Christianity and urged tolerance rather than persecu-tion of Christians. Bridging more than 1600 years Codex Sinaiticus is a vivid testament to human invention and spiritual inspiration.

As will become apparent from what follows, the survival of Codex Sinaiticus is a near miracle. The continued preservation of such a critical part of the Greek written heritage is a major responsibility of present and future generations.

WHAT IS CODEX SINAITICUS?

As it survives today, Codex Sinaiticus comprises just over 400 large leaves of prepared animal skin, partly calf, each of which measures 380 mm tall and 345 mm wide. On these parchment leaves is written around half of the Old Testament and Apocrypha, the whole of the New Testament, and two early Christian texts not found in modern Bibles, an Epistle ascribed to the Apostle Barnabas, and the Shepherd by the early 2nd-century Roman writer Hermas. All these texts are in Greek: the New Testament appears in the original vernacular language (*koinē*) and the Old Testament in the version that was adopted by early Greek-speaking Christians and has long been known as the Septuagint. Among the Old Testament books regarded in the West as apocryphal are 2 Esdras, Tobit, Judith, 1 & 4 Maccabees, Wisdom, and Sirach. Within the New Testament the Letter to the Hebrews is placed after Paul's Second Letter to the Thessalonians, and the Acts of the Apostles between the Pastoral and Catholic Epistles. Based principally on an analysis of the handwriting, known as palaeographical evidence, the Codex is generally dated to the 4th century, and sometimes more precisely to the middle of that century.

As presented in the Codex, the texts have an austere appearance, written entirely in capital letters and without word division (*scriptio continua*). Text breaks are indicated with the greatest of restraint and with very little punctuation. The beginning of each book of the Bible is marked only by its placement at the top of a new column and by the slight enlargement of the initial letter. The end of each book, which traditionally was given more prominence than the beginning in books of the

The Monastery of St Catherine, Mount Sinai, from *Ordnance Survey of the Peninsula of Sinai* (Southampton, 1869)

[5]

ΛΕΓΟΝΤΕϹΟΦΕΛΟΝ
ΑΠΕΘΑΝΟΜΕΝΤΗ
ΑΠΩΛΕΙΑΤΩΝΑΔΕΛ
ΦΩΝΗΜΩΝΕΝΑΝ
ΤΙΚΥΚΑΙΙΝΑΤΙΑΝΗ
ΓΑΓΕΤΑΙΤΗΝϹΥΝΑ
ΓΩΓΗΝΚΥΕΙϹΤΗΝΕ
ΡΗΜΟΝΤΑΥΤΗΝΑ
ΠΟΚΤΙΝΑΙΗΜΑϹΚΑΙ
ΤΑΚΤΗΝΗΗΜΩΝΚΑΙ
ΙΝΑΤΙΑΝΗΓΑΓΕΤΑΙ
ΗΜΑϹΕΞΑΙΓΥΠΤΟΥ
ΠΑΡΑΓΕΝΕϹΘΑΙΕΙϹ
ΤΟΝΤΟΠΟΝΤΟΝΠΟΝΗ
ΡΟΝΤΟΥΤΟΝΤΟΠΟϹ
ΟΥϹΠΕΙΡΕΤΑΙΟΥΤΑ
ϹΥΚΑΙΟΥΔΕΑΜΠΕΛΟΙ
ΟΥΔΕΡΟΑΙΟΥΔΕΥ
ΔΩΡΕϹΤΙΝΠΙΕΙΝ:
ΚΑΙΗΛΘΕΝΜΩΥϹΗϹ
ΚΑΙΑΑΡΩΝΑΠΟ
ΠΡΟϹΩΠΟΥΤΗϹϹΥ
ΝΑΓΩΓΗϹΕΠΙΤΗΝ
ΘΥΡΑΝΤΗϹϹΚΗΝΗϹ
ΤΟΥΜΑΡΤΥΡΙΟΥΚΑΙ
ΕΠΕϹΑΝΕΠΙΠΡΟ
ϹΩΠΟΝΚΑΙΩΦΘΗ
ΗΔΟΞΑΚΥΠΡΟϹΑΥ
ΤΟΥϹΚΑΙΕΛΑΛΗϹΕΝ
ΚϹΠΡΟϹΜΩΥϹΗΝ
ΛΕΓΩΝΛΑΒΕΤΗΝ
ΡΑΒΔΟΝΚΑΙΕΚΚΛΗ
ϹΙΑϹΟΝΤΗΝϹΥΝΑΓΩ
ΓΗΝϹΥΚΑΙΑΑΡΩΝ
ΟΑΔΕΛΦΟϹϹΟΥΚΑΙ
ΛΑΛΗϹΑΤΕΠΡΟϹΤΗΝ
ΠΕΤΡΑΝΕΝΑΝΤΙΟΝ
ΑΥΤΩΝΚΑΙΔΩϹΕΙ
ΤΑΥΔΑΤΑΑΥΤΗϹΚΑΙΕ
ΞΟΙϹΕΤΑΙΑΥΤΟΙϹΥ
ΔΩΡΕΚΤΗϹΠΕΤΡΑϹ
ΚΑΙΠΟΤΙΕΙΤΑΙΤΗΝ
ϹΥΝΑΓΩΓΗΝΚΑΙΤΑ
ΚΤΗΝΗΑΥΤΩΝ:
ΚΑΙΕΛΑΒΕΝΜΩΥϹΗϹ
ΤΗΝΡΑΒΔΟΝΤΗΝ
ΑΠΕΝΑΝΤΙΚΥΚΑ
ΘΑϹΥΝΕΤΑΞΕΝΚϹ

ΚΑΙΕΞΕΚΚΛΗϹΙΑϹΕ
ΜΩΥϹΗϹΚΑΙΑΑ
ΡΩΝΤΗΝϹΥΝΑΓΩ
ΓΗΝΑΠΕΝΑΝΤΙΤΗϹ
ΠΕΤΡΑϹΚΑΙΕΙΠΕΝ
ΠΡΟϹΑΥΤΟΥϹΑΚΟΥ
ϹΑΤΕΜΟΥΟΙΑΠΙΘΟΙ
ΜΗΕΚΤΗϹΠΕΤΡΑϹ
ΤΑΥΤΗϹΕΞΑΞΩΜΕΝΥΜΙΝ
ΥΔΩΡ·ΚΑΙΕΠΑΡΑϹ
ΜΩΥϹΗϹΤΗΝΧΙ
ΡΑΑΥΤΟΥΕΠΑΤΑΞΕ
ΤΗΝΠΕΤΡΑΝΡΑΒΔΩΔΙϹ
ΚΑΙΕΞΗΛΘΕΝΥΔΩΡ
ΠΟΛΥΚΑΙΕΠΙΕΝΗ
ϹΥΝΑΓΩΓΗΚΑΙΤΑ
ΚΤΗΝΗΑΥΤΩΝ:
ΚΑΙΕΙΠΕΝΚϹΠΡΟϹ
ΜΩΥϹΗΝΚΑΙΑΑΡΩΝ
ΟΤΙΟΥΚΕΠΙϹΤΕΥ
ϹΑΤΕΑΓΙΑϹΑΙΜΕ
ΝΑΝΤΙΟΝΥΙΩΝΙΗΛ
ΔΙΑΤΟΥΤΟΟΥΚΕΙϹΑ
ΞΕΤΕΥΜΕΙϹΕΙϹΤΗΝ
ϹΥΝΑΓΩΓΗΝΤΑΥ
ΤΗΝΕΙϹΤΗΝΓΗΝ
ΗΝΔΕΔΩΚΑΑΥΤΟΙϹ
ΤΟΥΤΟΤΟΥΔΩΡΑΝ
ΤΙΛΟΓΙΑϹΟΤΙΕΛΟΙ
ΔΟΡΗΘΗϹΑΝΟΙΥΙ
ΟΙΙΗΛΕΝΑΝΤΙΚΥ
ΚΑΙΗΓΙΑϹΘΗΑΥ
ΤΟΙϹΚϹ:
ΚΑΙΑΠΕϹΤΙΛΕΝΜΩ
ΥϹΗϹΑΓΓΕΛΟΥϹΕΚ
ΚΑΔΗϹΠΡΟϹΒΑϹΙ
ΛΕΑΕΔΩΜΛΕΓΩΝ
ΤΑΔΕΛΕΓΕΙΟΑΔΕΛ
ΦΟϹϹΟΥΙΗΛϹΥΕ
ΠΙϹΤΗΠΑΝΤΑΤΟΝ
ΜΟΧΘΟΝΤΟΝΕΥΡΟΝ
ΤΑΗΜΑϹΚΑΙΚΑΤΕ
ΒΗϹΑΝΟΙΠΑΤΕΡΕϹΗ
ΜΩΝΕΙϹΑΙΓΥΠΤΟΝ
ΚΑΙΠΑΡΩΚΗϹΑ
ΜΕΝΕΝΑΙΓΥΠΤΩ
ΗΜΕΡΑϹΠΛΕΙΟΥϹΚ
ΕΚΑΚΩϹΑΝΗΜΑϹ

ΟΙΑΙΓΥΠΤΙΟΙΚΑΙΤΟΥϹ
ΠΑΤΕΡΑϹΗΜΩΝΚΑΙ
ΑΝΕΚΟΗϹΑΜΕΝΠΡΟϹ
ΚΝΚΑΙΕΙϹΗΚΟΥϹΕ
ΚϹΤΗϹΦΩΝΗϹΗ
ΜΩΝΚΑΙΑΠΟϹΤΙ
ΛΑϹΑΓΓΕΛΟΝΕΞΗ
ΓΑΓΕΝΗΜΑϹΕΞΑΙ
ΓΥΠΤΟΥΚΑΙΝΥΝΕ
ΚΑΘΙϹΑΜΕΝΕΝΚΑ
ΔΗϹΠΟΛΕΙΕΚΜΕ
ΡΟΥϹΤΩΝΟΡΙΩΝ
ϹΟΥ·ΠΑΡΕΛΕΥϹΟΜΕ
ΘΑΔΙΑΤΗϹΓΗϹϹΟΥ
ΟΥΔΙΕΛΕΥϹΟΜΕΘΑ
ΔΙΑΓΡΩΝΟΥΔΕΔΙ
ΑΜΠΕΛΩΝΩΝΟΥ
ΔΕΠΙΟΜΕΘΑΥΔΩΡ
ΕΚΛΑΚΚΟΥϹΟΥΟ
ΔΩΒΑϹΙΛΙΚΗΠΟ
ΡΕΥϹΟΜΕΘΑΟΥΚΕΚ
ΚΛΙΝΟΥΜΕΝΔΕΞΙ
ΑΟΥΔΕΑΡΙϹΤΕΡΑΕ
ΩϹΑΝΠΑΡΕΛΘΩ
ΜΕΝΤΑΟΡΙΑϹΟΥ
ΚΑΙΕΙΠΕΝΠΡΟϹΑΥ
ΤΟΝΟΥΔΙΕΛΕΥϹΗ
ΔΙΕΜΟΥΕΙΔΕΜΗΕ
ΠΟΛΕΜΩΕΞΕΛΕΥ
ϹΟΜΕΘΑΕΙϹϹΥΝΑΝ
ΤΗϹΙΝϹΟΙΚΑΙΛΕΓΟΥ
ϹΙΝΑΥΤΩΟΙΥΙΟΙ
ΙΗΛΠΑΡΑΤΟΟΡΟϹ
ΠΑΡΕΛΕΥϹΟΜΕΘΑ
ΕΑΝΔΕΤΟΥΥΔΑΤΟϹ
ϹΟΥΠΙΩΜΕΝΕΓΩ
ΤΕΚΑΙΤΑΚΤΗΝΗΜΟΥ
ΔΩϹΩΤΙΜΗΝΑΛ
ΛΑΤΟΠΡΑΓΜΑΟΥΔΕ
ΕϹΤΙΝΠΑΡΑΤΟΟΡΟϹ
ΠΑΡΕΛΕΥϹΟΜΕΘΑ
ΟΔΕΕΙΠΕΝΟΥΔΙΕ
ΛΕΥϹΗΔΙΕΜΟΥ:
ΚΑΙΕΞΗΛΘΕΝΕΔΩΜ
ΕΙϹϹΥΝΑΝΤΗϹΙΝΑΥ
ΤΩΕΝΟΧΛΩΒΑΡΕΙ
ΚΑΙΕΝΧΙΡΙΙϹΧΥΡΑ
ΚΑΙΟΥΚΗΘΕΛΗϹΕΝ

ΕΔΩΜΔΟΥΝΑΙΤΟΝ
ΙϹΛΠΑΡΕΛΘΕΙΝΔΙ
ΑΤΩΝΟΡΙΩΝΑΥ
ΤΟΥ·ΚΑΙΕΞΕΚΛΙΝΕ
ΙϹΛΑΠΑΥΤΟΥ·ΚΑΙ
ΑΠΗΡΑΝΕΚΚΑΔΗ
ΚΑΙΠΑΡΕΓΕΝΟΝ
ΤΟΟΙΥΙΟΙΙΗΛΠΑϹΑ
ΗϹΥΝΑΓΩΓΗΕΙ
ΚΑΙΕΙΠΕΝΚϹΠΡΟϹ
ΜΩΥϹΗΝΚΑΙΑΑ
ΡΩΝ·ΕΝΩΡ·ΤΩΟ
ΡΕΙ·ΕΠΙΤΩΝΟΡΙΩΝ
ΓΗϹΕΔΩΜΛΕΓΩ
ΠΡΟϹΤΕΘΗΤΩΑ
ΑΡΩΝΠΡΟϹΤΟΝ
ΛΑΟΝΑΥΤΟΥΟΤΙΟΥ
ΜΗΕΙϹΕΛΘΗΤΕΕΙϹ
ΓΗΝ·ΗΝΔΕΔΩΚΑ
ΤΟΙϹΥΙΟΙϹΙϹΛΔΙΟ
ΤΙΠΑΡΩΞΥΝΑΤΕ
ΜΕΕΠΙΤΟΥΥΔΑΤ
ΤΗϹΛΟΙΔΟΡΙΑϹ
ΛΑΒΕΤΟΝΑΑΡΩ
ΚΑΙΕΛΕΑΖΑΡΤΟ
ΥΙΟΝΑΥΤΟΥΚΑΙΑ
ΝΑΒΙΒΑϹΟΝΑΥ
ΕΙϹΩΡ·ΤΟΟΡΟϹ
ΕΝΑΝΤΙΠΑϹΗϹΤ
ϹΥΝΑΓΩΓΗϹΚΑΙ
ΑΥϹΟΝΤΑΑΡΩΝΤ
ΕϹΤΟΛΗΝΑΥΤΟΥΚ
ΕΝΔΥϹΟΝΕΛΕΑΖ
ΤΟΝΥΙΟΝΑΥΤΟΥ
ΑΑΡΩΝΠΡΟϹΤΕΘ
ΑΠΟΘΑΝΕΤΩΕΚ
ΚΑΙΕΠΟΙΗϹΕΝ
ΜΩΥϹΗϹΚΑΘΑ
ΝΕΤΑΞΕΝΑΥΤΩ
ΚΑΙΑΝΕΒΙΒΑϹΕΝ
ΑΥΤΟΝΕΙϹΩΡ·Τ
ΟΡΟϹΕΝΑΝΤΙΟΝ
ϹΗϹϹΥΝΑΓΩΓΗ
ΕΞΕΔΥϹΕΝΑΑΡΩΝ
ΤΑΙΜΑΤΙΑΑΥΤΟΥ
ΚΑΙΕΝΕΔΥϹΕΝΑ
ΤΑΕΛΕΑΖΑΡΤΟΝ
ΥΙΟΝΑΥΤΟΥΚΑΙ

ancient Mediterranean world and included the title, is highlighted by two intersecting horizontal and vertical lines penned in the same ink as the main text and embellished with the simplest of decoration, sometimes in red ink. Apart from the titles to the Psalms and the Song of Solomon and the numbering in the Psalms and Gospels, which are executed in red ink, all the text of the Codex is written in shades of brown and nearly black ink, comprising an iron compound with some carbon.

Two features render pages of the Codex instantly recognisable. First, the Codex is unique among surviving Greek bound manuscripts in the arrangement of the majority of its text in four imposing narrow columns on each page. Indeed, when seen open, the Codex makes its initial impact on the viewer through the eight columns that shape most of its openings. In the layout of its text it has parallels only in the earlier rolls bearing non-Christian sacred writings or classic texts such as Homer's Odyssey, which when unrolled for reading revealed a succession of vertical columns set across the roll from left to right. Only the verse text of the poetical books of the Old Testament is laid out in the two-column format that was to become one of the standard means of presenting text on wide pages. Whereas the columns immediately impose themselves upon the viewer, the second distinctive feature requires more careful examination of the Codex. For within and around these columns of text it is possible to distinguish on almost every page some of the thousands of corrections that continue to fascinate scholars of the text of the Bible. Ranging in date from the 4th to the 12th century and in extent from the alteration of one letter to the insertion of whole sentences, some are easily observable in the margins and between the columns, whilst others

Codex Sinaiticus. Numbers 20:3-26, including the passage describing how Moses struck the rock with his staff, and waters streamed forth for the children of Israel. Monastery of St Catherine, Mount Sinai, New Finds, Majuscule MS 1

[7]

may also be identified on closer examination within the columns. No other early manuscript of the Christian Bible has been so extensively corrected.

Codex Sinaiticus, or the Book from Sinai, is named after the Monastery of St Catherine, Mount Sinai, the longest continuously active Christian monastic community. Tracing its origins back to the 4th century, this community was established around the site where, according to the book of Exodus, the patriarch Moses encountered God in the Burning Bush, at the foot of Mount Sinai in Egypt. By the middle of the 6th century the Emperor Justinian had established a fortified monastery there. Later, this monastery was dedicated to St Catherine of Alexandria, a Christian martyr whose remains are believed to have been transported miraculously to the site. Although the Codex probably formed part of the monastery's possessions from an early date, only eleven leaves and a few fragments, all from the beginning and end of the Codex, remain there to this day. The principal surviving portion, comprising 347 leaves, is now held by the British Library. A further 43 leaves, preserving two discrete parts of the Old Testament, are kept at the University Library in Leipzig and parts of five leaves at the National Library of Russia in St Petersburg. It is estimated that around 330 further leaves originally formed part of the Codex and completed the Old Testament. These leaves, which included most of the Old Testament before 1 Chronicles, as well as a large part of the Prophetic Books, are now untraced and presumed lost.

Codex Sinaiticus. Genesis 23:19 – 24:14, describing how Abraham found a wife for his son Isaac. St Petersburg, National Library of Russia, MS gr. 259, f. 1

Column 1

ΚΥΠΗΕCΤΙΝΧΕΒΕ
ΕΝΤΗΓΗΧΑΝΑΑΝ
ΚΛΕΝΥΦΩΝΟΛ
ΠΡΟΚΑΤΟCΤΙΝΛΑ
ΟΝΟΗΝΕΝΑΥΤΩ
ΤΩΑΒΡΑΑΜΕΙCΤΙ
CΙΝΤΑΦΟΥΠΑΡΑ
ΤΩΝΥΙΩΝΧΕΤ
ΚΑΙΑΚΡΑΑΜΗΝΤΗ
CΚΥΤΕΡΟCΠΡΟΚΕ
ΝΗΚΩCΤΗΓΚΩΝ
ΚΑΙΚCΕΥΛΟΓΗCΕ
ΤΟΝΑΒΡΑΑΜΚΑΤΑ
ΠΑΝΤΑ
ΚΑΙΕΙΠΕΝΑΒΡΑΑΜ
ΤΩΠΑΙΔΙΑΥΤΟΥ
ΤΩΠΡΕCΒΥΤΕΡΩ
ΤΗCΟΙΚΙΑCΑΥΤΤ
ΤΩΑΡΧΟΝΤΙΠΑΝ
ΤΩΝ ΤΩΝΑΥΤΟΥ
ΘΕCΤΗΝΧΕΙΡΑC
COΥΥΠΟΤΟΝΜΗ
ΜΟΥ·ΚΑΙΕΞΟΡΚΙΩ
CΕΚΝΤΟΝΟΝΤΟΥ
ΟΥΡΑΝΟΥΚΑΙΤΟΝ
ΟΝΤΗCΓΗCΙΝΑ
ΜΗΛΑΚΗCΓΥΝΑΙ
ΚΑΤΩΥΙΩΜΟΥ
CΑΑΚΑΠΟΤΩΝΘΥ
ΓΑΤΕΡΩΝΤΩΝΧΑ
ΝΑΝΑΙΩΝΜΕΘΩ
ΓΩΟΙΚΩΑΛΛΑ
ΕΙΝΜΟΥ

Column 2

ΕΙCΤΗΝΓΗΝΜΟΥΘΕ
ΕCΗΛΑΟΘΕΚΕΙΘΘ
ΕΠΕΝΛΕΙΨΩΤ
ΤΟΝΑΒΡΑΑΜΠ
ΕΧΕCΕΛΥΤΩΜΗ
ΑΠΟCΤΡΕΨΗCΤ
ΤΙΟΝΜΟΥΕΚΕΙ
ΚCΟΟCΤΟΥΟΥΡΑ
ΝΟΥΚΜΟΟCΤΗC
ΓΗCΟCΕΛΑΒΕΝΜΕ
ΤΗCΟΙΚΟΥ ΤΟΥ
ΠΑΤΡΟCΜΟΥ ΤΟΥ
ΕΚΤΗCΓΗCΗΓΕΝΝ
ΝΗΘΗΝΟCΕΛΑΛΗ
CΕΝΜΟΙΚΑΙΩΜΟ
CΕΝΤΟΙCΛΕΓΩΝ
CΠΕΡΜΑΤΙCΟΥΔ
ΤΗΝΓΗΝΤΑΥΤΗ
ΑΥΤΟCΑΠΟCΤΕΛΕΙ
ΑΥΤΟΥΕΜΠΡΟCΘΕ
COΥΚΑΙΛΗΜΨΗΓΥ
ΝΑΙΚΑΤΩΥΙΩΜΟΥ
ΕΚΕΙΘΕΝΕΑΝΔΕΜΗ
ΘΕΛΗCΗΓΥΝΗΠΟ
ΘΗΝΑΙΔΙΕΤΑCΟΥ
ΚΑΘΑΡΟCΕCΗΑΠΟ
ΤΗCΟΡΚΟΥ ΤΟΥΤ
ΜΟΝΟΝΤΟΝ
ΜΟΥΜΗ

Column 3

CΕΙCΤΗΝΓΗΝΤΑΥ
ΧΩΡΑΝΤΟΥΗC
ΤΗΡΑΛΛΟΓΕCC
CΤΗΝΜΕΝΝ
ΕΛΙΘΕΝΤΟΠΡΟC
ΤΟΥΚΥΡΙΟΥΜΟΥ
ΑΒΡΑΑΜΤΟΥΤ
ΤΗC
ΤΩΝ ΤΩΝ
ΓΤΤΩΝ ΤΑΝ
ΤΗΓ ΤΟΤΕCΤΙ
ΤΗΝΤΕΝ
ΚΑΙΤΟΥΤΩΝ
ΤΩΝ ΤΩΝ ΑΓΑΘ
ΓΤΩΝ ΝΟΓΡCΤΙ
ΤΗΓΤΤΤΤΝΤΑ

THE SIGNIFICANCE OF CODEX SINAITICUS

It is important to have a clear understanding of Codex Sinaiticus in the context of all the manuscripts of parts of the Bible that survive and underpin the many editions, translations, and versions read by Christians across the world today. First, only one other nearly complete manuscript of the Christian Bible is of a similarly early date. Housed in the Vatican Library in Rome, the Codex Vaticanus preserves a much larger part of the Old Testament than Codex Sinaiticus, but is incomplete in the New Testament. It is generally acknowledged to be closely related to Codex Sinaiticus. Indeed some scholars have argued that the same scribe worked on both manuscripts. Differing opinions are held on which is the older manuscript and only further research will resolve this matter conclusively.

Second, the only Christian manuscripts of scripture that are definitely of an earlier date than Sinaiticus contain relatively small portions of text. Written mainly on papyrus, the paper of the Graeco-Roman world, these manuscripts preserve parts of small-format books, comparable in size to modern pocket paperbacks, that contained only one or a handful of Greek texts. These books were written not by professional book-scribes, but rather by those used to writing text for documents. The surviving parchment leaves bearing part of the Christian Bible are less than half the size of those of Sinaiticus, with the text generally written in one column. None appears to have formed part of a manuscript of the whole Old or New Testaments, let alone the whole Bible.

Third, strikingly few traces remain of parchment codices produced before Codex Sinaiticus. Only seven parchment codices of parts of the

Codex Vaticanus. Conclusion of the Gospel of Luke and beginning of the Gospel of John. Biblioteca Apostolica Vaticana, MS gr. 1209, p. 1349.

+   +   + 1399

Column 1

ΝΒ ΤΑΣΓΡΑΦΑΣ ΚΑΙΑΝΑ
ΣΤΑΝΤΕΣΑΥΤΗΤΗΩΡΑ
ΥΠΕΣΤΡΕΨΑΝΕΙΣΙΕΡΟΥ
ΣΑΛΗΜΚΑΙΕΥΡΟΝΗΘ
ΣΜΕΝΟΥΣΤΟΥΣΕΝΔΕΚΑ
ΚΑΙΤΟΥΣΣΥΝΑΥΤΟΙΣΛΕ
ΓΟΝΤΑΣΟΤΙΟΝΤΩΣΗΓΕΡ
ΘΗΟΚΣΚΑΙΩΦΘΗΣΙΜΩ
ΝΙΚΑΙΑΥΤΟΙΣΕΞΗΓΟΥΝ
ΤΑΕΝΤΗΟΔΩΚΑΙΩΣΕΓ
ΣΘΗΑΥΤΟΙΣΕΝΤΗΚΛΑ
ΣΕΙΤΟΥΑΡΤΟΥΤΑΥΤΑ
ΔΕΑΥΤΩΝΛΑΛΟΥΝΤΩ
ΑΥΤΟΣΕΣΤΗΕΝΜΕΣΩΑΥ
ΤΩΝΚΑΙΛΕΓΕΙΑΥΤΟΙΣΕΙ
ΡΗΝΗΥΜΙΝ ΘΡΟΗΘΕΝΤΕ
ΔΕΚΑΙΕΜΦΟΒΟΙΓΕΝΟΜΕ
ΝΟΙΕΔΟΚΟΥΝΠΝΕΥΜΑ
ΘΕΩΡΕΙΝ ΚΑΙΕΙΠΕΝΑΥ
ΤΙΤΕΤΑΡΑΓΜΕΝΟΙΕΣΤΕ
ΚΑΙΤΙΔΙΑΛΟΓΙΣΜΟΙΑΝΑ
ΒΑΙΝΟΥΣΙΝΕΝΤΗΚΑΡΔΙ
ΑΥΜΩΝΙΔΕΤΕΤΑΣΧΕΙ
ΡΑΣΜΟΥΚΑΙΤΟΥΣΠΟΔΑ
ΜΟΥΟΤΙΕΓΩΕΙΜΙΑΥΤΟΣ
ΨΗΛΑΦΗΣΑΤΕΜΕΚΑΙ
ΔΕΤΕΟΤΙΠΝΕΥΜΑΚΑΙ
ΣΑΡΚΑΚΑΙΟΣΤΕΑΟΥΚΕ
ΧΕΙΚΑΘΩΣΕΜΕΘΕΩΡΕΙ
ΤΕΕΧΟΝΤΑ ΚΑΙΤΟΥΤΟ
ΕΙΠΩΝΕΔΕΙΞΕΝΑΥΤΟΙΣ
ΤΑΣΧΕΙΡΑΣΚΑΙΤΟΥΣΠΟ
ΔΑΣΕΤΙΔΕΑΠΙΣΤΟΥΝ
ΤΩΝΑΠΟΤΗΣΧΑΡΑ
ΚΑΙΘΑΥΜΑΖΟΝΤΩΝΕΙΠΕ
ΑΥΤΟΙΣΕΧΕΤΕΤΙΒΡΩ
ΜΟΝΕΝΘΑΔΕ ΟΙΔΕΕΠΕ
ΔΩΚΑΝΑΥΤΩΙΧΘΥΟΣ
ΟΠΤΟΥΜΕΡΟΣΚΑΙΛΑΒΩ
ΕΝΩΠΙΟΝΑΥΤΩΝΕΦΑ
ΓΕΝ ΕΙΠΕΝΔΕΠΡΟΣΑΥ
ΤΟΥΣΟΥΤΟΙΟΙΛΟΓΟΙΜΟΥ

Column 2

ΟΥΣΕΛΑΛΗΣΑΠΡΟΣΥΜΑΣ
ΕΤΙΩΝΣΥΝΥΜΙΝΟΤΙΔΕ
ΠΛΗΡΩΘΗΝΑΙΑΠΑΝΤΑ
ΤΑΓΕΓΡΑΜΜΕΝΑΕΝΤΩ
ΝΟΜΩΜΩΥΣΕΩΣΚΑΙΤΟΙΣ
ΠΡΟΦΗΤΑΙΣΚΑΙΨΑΛΜ
ΠΕΡΙΕΜΟΥ ΤΟΤΕΔΙΗΝ
ΞΕΝΑΥΤΩΝΤΟΝΝΟΥΝ
ΤΟΥΣΥΝΕΙΝΑΙΤΑΣΓΡΑ
ΦΑΣ ΚΑΙΕΙΠΕΝΑΥΤΟΙΣ
ΟΤΙΟΥΤΩΣΓΕΓΡΑΠΤΑΙ
ΠΑΘΕΙΝΤΟΝΧΝΚΑΙΑΝΑ
ΣΤΗΝΑΙΕΚΝΕΚΡΩΝΤΗ
ΤΡΙΤΗΗΜΕΡΑΚΑΙΚΗΡΥ
ΧΘΗΝΑΙΕΠΙΤΩΟΝΟΜΑ
ΤΙΑΥΤΟΥΜΕΤΑΝΟΙΑΝ
ΕΙΣΑΦΕΣΙΝΑΜΑΡΤΙΩΝ
ΕΙΣΠΑΝΤΑΤΑΕΘΝΗΑΡ
ΞΑΜΕΝΟΙΑΠΟΙΕΡΟΥΣΑ
ΛΗΜ ΥΜΕΙΣΜΑΡΤΥΡΕΣ
ΤΟΥΤΩΝ ΚΑΙΙΔΟΥΕΓΩ
ΕΞΑΠΟΣΤΕΛΛΩΤΗΝΕ
ΠΑΓΓΕΛΙΑΝΤΟΥΠΑΤΡ
ΜΟΥΕΦΥΜΑΣΥΜΕΙΣΔΕ
ΚΑΘΙΣΑΤΕΕΝΤΗΠΟΛΕΙ
ΕΩΣΟΥΕΝΔΥΣΗΣΘΕΕΞ
ΥΟΥΣΑΔΥΝΑΜΙΝ ΕΞΗΓΑ
ΓΕΝΔΕΑΥΤΟΥΣΕΩΣΠΡ
ΒΗΘΑΝΙΑΝΚΑΙΕΠΑΡΑΣ
ΤΑΣΧΕΙΡΑΣΑΥΤΟΥΕΥΛΟ
ΓΗΣΕΝΑΥΤΟΥΣΚΑΙΕΓΕ
ΝΕΤΟΕΝΤΩΕΥΛΟΓΕΙΝ
ΑΥΤΟΝΑΥΤΟΥΣΔΙΕΣΤΗ
ΑΠΑΥΤΩΝΚΑΙΑΝΕΦΕ
ΡΕΤΟΕΙΣΤΟΝΟΥΡΑΝΟΝΚ
ΑΥΤΟΙΠΡΟΣΚΥΝΗΣΑΝ
ΤΕΣΑΥΤΟΝΥΠΕΣΤΡΕ
ΕΙΣΙΕΡΟΥΣΑΛΗΜΜΕΤ
ΧΑΡΑΣΚΑΙΗΣΑΝΔΙΑΠΑΝΤ
ΕΝΤΩΙΕΡΩΕΥΛΟΓΟΥ
ΤΕΣΤΟΝΘΝΑΜΗΝ

ΚΑΤΑ ΛΟΥΚΑΝ

Column 3

ΕΝΑΡΧΗΗΝΟΛΟΓΟΣΚΑΙ
ΟΛΟΓΟΣΗΝΠΡΟΣΤΟΝΘΝ
ΚΑΙΘΣΗΝΟΛΟΓΟΣ ΟΥΤΟΣ
ΗΝΕΝΑΡΧΗΠΡΟΣΤΟΝΘΝ
ΠΑΝΤΑΔΙΑΥΤΟΥΕΓΕΝΕ
ΤΟΚΑΙΧΩΡΙΣΑΥΤΟΥΕΓΕ
ΝΕΤΟΟΥΔΕΕΝΟΓΕΓΟ
ΕΝΑΥΤΩΖΩΗΗΝΚΑΙ
ΖΩΗΗΝΤΟΦΩΣΚΑΙΤΟ
ΦΩΣΕΝΤΗΣΚΟΤΙΑΦΑΙ
ΝΕΙΚΑΙΗΣΚΟΤΙΑΑΥΤ
ΟΥΚΑΤΕΛΑΒΕΝ ΕΓΕΝΕ
ΤΟΑΝΘΡΩΠΟΣΑΠΕΣΤΑΛ
ΜΕΝΟΣΠΑΡΑΘΥΟΝΟΜΑ
ΑΥΤΩΙΩΑΝΗΣΟΥΤΟΣ
ΗΛΘΕΝΕΙΣΜΑΡΤΥΡΙΑΝ
ΙΝΑΜΑΡΤΥΡΗΣΗΠΕΡΙΤΟ
ΦΩΤΟΣΙΝΑΠΑΝΤΕΣΠΙ
ΣΤΕΥΣΩΣΙΝΔΙΑΥΤΟΥ
ΟΥΚΗΝΕΚΕΙΝΟΣΤΟΦΩ
ΑΛΛΙΝΑΜΑΡΤΥΡΗΣΗΠΕ
ΡΙΤΟΥΦΩΤΟΣ ΗΝΤΟΦΩ
ΤΟΑΛΗΘΕΙΝΟΝΟΦΩΤΙ
ΖΕΙΠΑΝΤΑΑΝΘΡΩΠΟΝ
ΕΡΧΟΜΕΝΟΝΕΙΣΤΟΝΚ
ΣΜΟΝ ΕΝΤΩΚΟΣΜΩΗΝ
ΚΑΙΟΚΟΣΜΟΣΔΙΑΥΤΟΥ
ΕΓΕΝΕΤΟΚΑΙΟΚΟΣΜΟΣ
ΑΥΤΟΝΟΥΚΕΓΝΩΕΙΣ
ΤΑΙΔΙΑΗΛΘΕΝΚΑΙΟΙΙ
ΟΙΑΥΤΟΝΟΥΠΑΡΕΛΑΒΟ
ΟΣΟΙΔΕΕΛΑΒΟΝΑΥΤΟΝ
ΕΔΩΚΕΝΑΥΤΟΙΣΕΞΟΥ
ΣΙΑΝΤΕΚΝΑΘΥΓΕΝΕΣΘΑΙ
ΤΟΙΣΠΙΣΤΕΥΟΥΣΙΝΕΙΣ
ΤΟΟΝΟΜΑΑΥΤΟΥΟΙΟΥ
ΚΕΞΑΙΜΑΤΩΝΟΥΔΕΕΚ
ΘΕΛΗΜΑΤΟΣΣΑΡΚΟΣΟΥΔ
ΑΛΛΕΚΘΥΕΓΕΝΝΗΘΗΣΑ
ΚΑΙΟΛΟΓΟΣΣΑΡΞΕΓΕΝ
ΤΟΚΑΙΕΣΚΗΝΩΣΕΝΕΝΗ
ΜΙΝΚΑΙΕΘΕΑΣΑΜΕΘΑ

(marginal note, right of column 2/3): ΤΩΝΑΝΘΡΩΠΩΝ

Bible definitely produced in a Christian context have any claim to date from before AD 300. Of these, four are complete single leaves containing parts of Tobit, John's Gospel, Acts and 2 John; three are mere fragments of leaves with Exodus, Luke's Gospel and Romans. Even if the period considered is extended to include the early 4th century, the total number of parchment leaves increases by only two, in the form of two fragments of Psalms and Hebrews. Moreover, out of all the surviving parchment codices datable to before AD 400 only two, Codex Vercellensis and Codex Bobiensis, preserve larger portions of the Christian Bible on parchment. The texts of these two manuscripts are Latin translations, not the original Greek, and even the larger one contains only the Four Gospels, not the whole New Testament nor the whole Bible. What greater contrast could there be than that between the total of nine stray parchment leaves of the Greek Bible produced before the middle of the 4th century and over one thousand preserved jointly by Codex Sinaiticus and Codex Vaticanus?

Unknown Gospel. These three fragments from a papyrus codex dating from the 1st half of the 2nd century are parts of one of the two earliest surviving Christian manuscripts. Their text relates a very early version of the Gospel story. British Library, Egerton Papyrus 2 verso

THE MAKING OF CODEX SINAITICUS

Codex Sinaiticus is a triumph of advanced technology. Even as they began their work, the producers of the volume faced huge challenges. A commitment to large pages of sometimes translucent fineness, almost certainly motivated by a desire to endow the sacred scriptures with a grandeur and sober luxury, required an extensive supply of high-quality parchment onto which to write the biblical text. For the complete Codex as many as 365 large animal skins would have been required, if, as seems likely, only one double-page spread could be made from one skin. Each of these skins needed to be assessed for quality and then carefully prepared before any writing could be undertaken. Laying out the text over so many vast pages also required the most careful planning; writing it down required skilled scribes capable of subsuming most of their individuality for the benefit of a harmonious overall appearance. A commitment to include in one volume so many texts, thus confirming the approved selection – or canon – of Christian scripture, required a large number of manuscripts of individual texts or smaller groups of texts from which to copy the text of the Codex. It also required the development of a substantial binding structure capable of supporting and containing within one volume over 730 large-format leaves. So much activity and text necessitated firm editorial control. It also involved significant costs. According to one calculation, the hours of labour taken in transcribing the text would have cost more than a top lawyer was allowed to earn from thirty cases, or a farm labourer, stone mason, carpenter, baker or writing master could earn in 6000 working days – in other words virtually a lifetime's wages for most people. The parchment on which the text was written could have cost half as much again.

As is the case with most other manuscripts of this antiquity, we do not know the identity of either the producers or the exact location in which they worked. Yet, some important facts can be deduced about the producers of the Codex and their place of work. First, it is possible to discern at least three different hands at work on the copying of the main text. Known to scholars as A, B and D, each of these three scribes brought to their task very different abilities in spelling and methods of concluding each book that they copied. Although trained to write in very similar ways, the three scribes also brought some individuality to their work, both in the execution of individual letters of the alphabet and in the presentation of the text. During the production of the Codex each corrected his own work, altering one or more letters in individual words and supplying words or passages omitted. At the end of John's Gospel Scribe A corrected his original text by erasing the closing design – or *coronis* – and the title, and adding in their place the concluding verse (John 21:25) 'And there are also many other things which Jesus did, the which, if they were to be written every one, I suppose that even the world itself could not contain the books that should be written', all followed by a new *coronis* and title. Significantly this final verse of John's Gospel has long been suspected by textual critics to be a later addition. The best of the scribes (D), who was responsible for copying parts of the Old Testament, also corrected and rewrote parts by the second-best scribe (A), who was responsible for other parts of the Old Testament and the entire New Testament apart from the first five verses of Revelation.

Overleaf
Codex Sinaiticus.
Conclusion of the
Gospel of John.
British Library, Add.
MS 43725, ff. 259v-260

[15]

ΠΟΥCΗCΕΙCΤΟΜΝΗ
ΜΕΙΟΝΚΑΙΒΛΕΠΕΙ
ΤΟΝΛΙΘΟΝΗΡΜΕΝ
ΑΠΟΤΗCΘΥΡΑCΕΚ
ΜΝΗΜΙΟΥΤΡΕΧΕΙ
ΚΑΙΕΡΧΕΤΑΙΠΡΟC
CΙΜΩΝΑΠΕΤΡΟΝ
ΚΑΙΠΡΟCΤΟΝΑΛΛΟΝ
ΜΑΘΗΤΗΝΟΝΕΦΙ
ΛΕΙΟΙCΚΑΙΛΕΓΕΙ
ΤΟΙCΗΡΑΝΤΟΝΚΝ
ΕΚΤΟΥΜΝΗΜΙΟΥΚΑΙ
ΟΥΚΟΙΔΑΜΕΝΠΟΥ
ΕΘΗΚΑΝΑΥΤΟΝΕΞΗΛ
ΘΕΝΟΥΝΟΠΕΤΡΟC
ΚΑΙΟΑΛΛΟCΜΑΘΗ
ΤΗCΚΑΙΗΡΧΟΝΤΟ
ΑΓΩΟΜΟΥΠΡΟC
ΔΡΑΜΕΝΔΕΤΑΧΙΟΝ
ΤΟΥΠΕΤΡΟΥΚΑΙΗΛ
ΘΕΝΕΙCΤΟΜΝΗΜΙ
ΠΡΩΤΟCΚΑΙΠΑΡΑ
ΤΑCΒΛΕΠΕΙΤΑΟΘΟ
ΝΙΑΚΕΙΜΕΝΑΚΑΙ
ΤΟCΟΥΛΑΡΙΟΝΟΗΝ
ΕΠΙΤΗCΚΕΦΑΛΗC
ΑΥΤΟΥΟΥΜΕΤΑΤΩΝ
ΟΘΟΝΙΩΝΚΕΙΜΕΝΟ
ΑΛΛΑΧΩΡΙCΕΝΤΥ
ΛΙΓΜΕΝΟΝΕΙCΕΝΑ
ΤΟΠΟΝΤΟΤΕΟΥΝ
ΕΙCΗΛΘΕΝΚΑΙΟΑΛ
ΛΟCΜΑΘΗΤΗCΟΑ
ΘΩΝΠΡΩΤΟCΕ
ΤΟΜΝΗΜΙΟΝΚΑΙ
ΕΙΔΕΝΚΑΙΕΠΙCΤΕ
CΕΝΟΥΔΕΠΩΓΑΡ
ΗΔΕΙCΑΝΤΗΝΓΡΑΦΗΝ
ΟΤΙΔΕΙΑΥΤΟΝΕΚ
ΝΕΚΡΩΝΑΝΑCΤΗΝΑΙ
ΑΠΗΛΘΟΝΟΥΝΠΑ
ΛΙΝΠΡΟCΑΥΤΟΥC
ΜΑΘΗΤΑΙΜΑΡΙΑΜ
ΔΕΙCΤΗΚΕΙΕΝΤΩ
ΜΝΗΜΙΩΚΛΑΙΟΥ
CΑΩCΟΥΝΕΚΛΑΙΕΝ
ΠΑΡΕΚΥΨΕΝΕΙC
ΜΝΗΜΙΟΝΚΑΙΘΙ

ΩΡΕΙΑΓΓΕΛΟΥCΚΑ
ΘΕΖΟΜΕΝΟΥCΕΝ
ΛΕΥΚΟΙCΕΝΑΠΡΟ
ΤΗΚΕΦΑΛΗΚΑΙΕ
ΝΑΠΡΟCΤΟΙCΠΟ
CΙΝΟΠΟΥΕΚΕΙΤΟΤΟ
CΩΜΑΤΟΥΙΥΛΕΓΟΥ
CΙΝΑΥΤΗΕΚΕΙΝΟΙ
ΓΥΝΑΙΤΙΚΛΑΙΕΙC
ΛΕΓΕΙΑΥΤΟΙCΟΤΙ Η
ΡΑΝΤΟΝΚΝΜΟΥΚΑΙ
ΟΥΚΟΙΔΑΠΟΥΕΘΗ
ΚΑΝΑΥΤΟΝ
ΤΑΥΤΑΕΙΠΟΥCΑΕCΤΡΑ
ΦΗΕΙCΤΑΟΠΙCΩΚΑΙ
ΘΕΩΡΕΙΤΟΝΙΝΕ
CΤΩΤΑΚΑΙΟΥΚΗΔΕΙ
ΟΤΙΙCΕCΤΙΝΛΕΓΕΙ
ΑΥΤΗΙCΓΥΝΑΙΤΙ
ΚΛΑΙΕΙCΤΙΝΑΖΗ
ΤΕΙCΕΚΕΙΝΗΔΕ
ΚΟΥCΑΟΤΙΟΚΗΠΟ
ΡΟCΕCΤΙΝΛΕΓΕΙΑΥ
ΤΩΚΕΕΙCΥΕΒΑ
CΤΑCΑCΑΥΤΟΝΕΙ
ΠΕΜΟΙΠΟΥΕΘΗ
ΚΑCΑΥΤΟΝΚΑΓΩ
ΤΟΝΑΡΩ
ΛΕΓΕΙΑΥΤΗΟΙCΜΑΡΙ
ΑΜCΤΡΑΦΕΙCΑΛΕ
ΚΕΙΝΗΛΕΓΕΙΑΥΤΩ
ΒΡΑΙCΤΙΡΑΒΒΟΥΝΙ
ΟΛΕΓΕΤΑΙΔΙΔΑCΚΑ
ΛΕΛΕΓΕΙΑΥΤΗΟΙC
ΜΗΜΟΥΑΠΤΟΥΟΥ
ΠΩΓΑΡΑΝΑΒΕΒΗ
ΚΑΠΡΟCΤΟΝΠΑΤΕ
ΡΑΠΟΡΕΥΟΥΔΕΠΡΟ
ΤΟΥCΑΔΕΛΦΟΥCΜΟ
ΕΙΠΕΑΥΤΟΙCΑΝΑ
ΒΑΙΝΩΠΡΟCΤΟΝ
ΠΑΤΕΡΑΜΟΥΚΑΙΠΑ
ΤΕΡΑΥΜΩΝΚΑΙΘΝ
ΜΟΥΚΑΙΘΝΥΜΩΝ
ΕΡΧΕΤΑΙΜΑΡΙΑΜΗ
ΜΑΓΔΑΛΗΝΗΑΓΓΕ
ΛΟΥCΑΤΟΙCΜΑΘΗΤΑΙC
ΟΤΙΕΩΡΑΚΑΤΟΝΚΝ

ΚΑΙΤΑΥΤΑΕΙΠΕΝΑΥ
ΤΗΟΥCΗCΟΥΝΟΨΙ
ΑCΤΗΗΜΕΡΑCΕΚΕΙ
ΝΗΜΙΑCΑΒΒΑΤΩΝ
ΚΑΙΤΩΝΘΥΡΩΝΚΕ
ΚΛΕΙCΜΕΝΩΝΟΠΟΥΗ
CΑΝΟΙΜΑΘΗΤΑΙ
ΔΙΑΤΟΝΦΟΒΟΝ
ΙΟΥΔΑΙΩΝΗΛΘΕΝ
ΟΙCΚΑΙΕCΤΗΕΙCΤΟ
ΜΕCΟΝΚΑΙΛΕΓΕΙ
ΝΗΥΜΙΝΚΑΙΤΟΥ
ΕΙΠΩΝΕΔΕΙΞΕΝΤΑ
ΧΙΡΑCΚΑΙΤΗΝΠΛΕΥ
ΡΑΝΑΥΤΟΙCΕΧΑΡΗ
CΑΝΟΙΜΑΘΗΤΑΙ
ΔΟΝΤΕCΤΟΝΚΝ
ΕΙΠΕΝΟΥΝΑΥΤΟΙC
ΠΑΛΙΝΕΙΡΗΝΗΥ
ΜΙΝΚΑΘΩCΑΠΕ
CΤΑΛΚΕΝΜΕΟΠΑ
ΤΗΡΚΑΓΩΠΕΜ
ΥΜΑCΚΑΙΤΟΥΤΟΕΙ
ΠΩΝΕΝΕΦΥCΗ
ΚΑΙΛΕΓΕΙΑΥΤΟΙC
ΛΑΒΕΤΕΠΝΑΑΓΙΟΝ
ΑΝΤΙΝΩΝΑΦΗΤΑΙ
ΤΑCΑΜΑΡΤΙΑCΑΦΕ
ΘΗCΕΤΑΙΑΥΤΟΙCΕ
ΑΝΛΕΤΙΝΩΝΚΡΑ
ΤΗΝΤΑΙΚΕΚΡΑΤΗΝ
ΤΑΙΘΩΜΑCΔΕΕΙ
ΕΚΤΩΝΔΩΔΕΚΑ
ΛΕΓΟΜΕΝΟCΔΙΔΥ
ΜΟCΟΥΚΗΝΜΕ
ΤΑΥΤΩΝΟΤΕΟΥΝΗΛ
ΘΕΝΙCΕΛΕΓΟΝΑΥ
ΤΩΟΙΜΑΘΗΤΑΙΕ
ΩΡΑΚΑΜΕΝΤΟΝ
ΚΝΟΔΕΕΙΠΕΝΑΥ
ΤΟΙCΕΑΝΜΗΙΔ
ΕΝΤΑΙCΧΕΡCΙΝ
ΤΥΠΟΝΤΩΝΗΛΩ
ΚΑΙΒΑΛΩΜΟΥΤΟΝ
ΔΑΚΤΥΛΟΝΕΙCΤΗΝ
ΧΕΙΡΑΝΑΥΤΟΥΚΑΙ
ΒΑΛΩΜΟΥΤΗΝΧΕΙ
ΡΑΕΙCΤΗΝΠΛΕΥΡΑ

ΑΥΤΟΥΟΥΜΗΠΙ
CΤΩΚΑΙΜΕΘΗΜΕ
ΡΑCΟΚΤΩΠΑΛΙΝ
ΗCΑΝΕCΩΟΙΜΑ
ΘΗΤΑΙΚΑΙΘΩΜΑC
ΜΕΤΑΥΤΩΝ
ΕΡΧΕΤΑΙΟΙCΤΩ
ΘΥΡΩΝΚΕΚΛΕΙCΜΕ
ΝΩΝΚΑΙΕCΤΗΕΙC
ΤΟΜΕCΟΝΚΑΙΕΙ
ΠΕΝΕΙΡΗΝΗΥΜΙ
ΕΙΤΑΛΕΓΕΙΤΩΘΩ
ΜΑΦΕΡΕΤΟΝΔΑ
ΚΤΥΛΟΝCΟΥΩΔΕ
ΚΑΙΙΔΕΤΑCΧΕΙΡΑC
ΜΟΥΚΑΙΦΕΡΕΤΗ
ΧΕΙΡΑCΟΥΚΑΙΒΑΛΕ
ΕΙCΤΗΝΠΛΕΥΡΑ
ΜΟΥΚΑΙΜΗΓΙΝΟΥ
ΑΠΙCΤΟCΑΛΛΑ
ΠΙCΤΟCΑΠΕΚΡΙΘΗΘΩ
ΜΑCΚΑΙΕΙΠΕΝ
ΑΥΤΩΟΚCΜΟΥΚΑΙ
ΟΘCΜΟΥΛΕΓΕΙ
ΑΥΤΩΟΙCΟΤΙ
ΕΩΡΑΚΑCΜΕΠΕ
ΠΙCΤΕΥΚΑCΜΑΚΑ
ΡΙΟΙΟΙΜΗΙΔΟΝ
ΤΕCΚΑΙΠΙCΤΕΥ
CΑΝΤΕCΠΟΛΛΑΜΕ
ΟΥΝΚΑΙΑΛΛΑCΗ
ΜΕΙΑΕΠΟΙΗCΕΝΟ
ΟΙCΕΝΩΠΙΟΝΤΩΝ
ΜΑΘΗΤΩΝΑΥΤΟΥ
ΑΟΥΚΕCΤΙΝΓΕ
ΓΡΑΜΜΕΝΑΕΝΤΩΒΙ
ΒΛΙΩΤΟΥΤΩΤΑΥ
ΤΑΔΕΓΕΓΡΑΠΤΑΙ
ΙΝΑΠΙCΤΕΥΗΤΕΟΤΙ
ΙCΕCΤΙΝΟΧCΟΥC
ΤΟΥΘΥΚΑΙΙΝΑΠΙCΤΕ
ΥΟΝΤΕCΖΩΗΝΕΧΗ
ΤΕΕΝΤΩΟΝΟΜΑ
ΤΙΑΥΤΟΥ
ΜΕΤΑΤΑΥΤΑΕΦΑ
ΝΕΡΩCΕΝΕΑΥΤΟΝΠΑΛΙΝ
ΟΙCΤΟΙCΜΑΘΗ
ΤΑΙCΕΠΙΤΗCΘΑ

CΗCΤΗCΤΙΒΕΡΙΑ···
ΕΦΑΝΕΡΩCΕΝΔΕ
ΟΥΤΩCΗCΑΝΟΜ·Ι
CΙΜΩΝΠΕΤΡΟCΚ
ΘΩΜΑCΟΛΕΓΟΜΕ
ΝΟCΔΙΔΥΜΟCΚΑΙ
ΝΑΘΑΝΑΗΛΟΑΠΟ
ΚΑΝΑΤΗCΓΑΛΙΛ
ΑCΚΑΙΟΙΥΙΟΙΖΕΒ
ΑΛΟΥΚΑΙΑΛΛΟΙΚ
ΤΩΝΜΑΘΗΤΩΝΑ
ΙΟΥΑΥΟ:
ΛΕΓΕΙΑΥΤΟΙCCΙΜΩ
ΠΕΤΡΟCΥΠΑΓΩΑ
ΛΙΕΥΕΙΝΛΕΓΟΥCΙΝ
ΑΥΤΩΕΡΧΟΜΕΘΑΚ
ΗΜΕΙCCΥΝCΟΙΕΞΗ
ΘΟΝΟΥΝΚΑΙΕΝΕ
ΒΗCΑΝΕΙCΤΟΠΛΟΙ
ΟΝΚΑΙΕΝΕΚΙΝΗΤΗ
ΝΥΚΤΙΕΠΙΑCΑΝΟΥ
ΔΥΕΝΠΡΩΙΑCΔΕΗ
ΕΝΟΜΕΝΗCΕCΤΗ
ΤΟΝΑΙΓΙΑΛΟΝ
ΟΥΜΕΝΤΟΙΕΓΝΩ
CΑΝΟΙΜΑΘΗΤΑΙΟΤ
ΙCΕCΤΙΝ·
ΛΕΓΕΙΟΥΝΑΥΤΟΙC
ΠΑΙΔΙΑΜΗΤΙΠΡΟC
ΦΑΓΙΟΝΕΧΕΤΕΑΠ
ΡΙΘΗCΑΝΑΥΤΩΟΥ·
ΛΕΓΕΙΑΥΤΟΙCΒΑΛ
ΕΤΕΙCΤΑΔΕΞΙΑΜΕ
ΡΗΤΟΥΠΛΟΙΟΥΤΟ
ΔΙΚΤΥΟΝΚΑΙΕΥΡΗ
ΕΤΕΟΙΔΕΕΒΑΛΟΝΚ
ΚΑΙΟΥΚΕΤΙΑΥΤΟ
ΥCΑΙΙCΧΥΟΝΑΠ
ΟΥΠΛΗΘΟΥCΤΩΝ
ΙΧΘΥΩΝ·ΛΕΓΕΙΟΤ
ΜΑΘΗΤΗCΕΚΕΙ
ΝΟCΟΝΗΓΑΠΑΟΙ
ΤΩΠΕΤΡΩΟΚCΕCΤΙ
Ν·CΙΜΩΝΟΥΝΠΕΤ
ΚΟΥCΑCΟΤΙΟΚC
CΤΙΝΤΟΝΕΠΕΝΔ
ΤΗΝΔΙΕΖΩCΑΤΟ
ΝΙΑΡΓΥΜΝΟCΙC

ΕΒΑΛΕΝΕΑΥΤΟΝ·Ι
ΤΗΝΘΑΛΑCCΑΝΟΙ
ΔΕΑΛΛΟΙΜΑΘΗΤΑ
ΤΩΠΛΟΙΑΡΙ
ΩΗΛΘΟΝ·ΟΥΓΑΡΗ
CΑΝΜΑΚΡΑΝΑΠΟ
ΤΗCΓΗCΑΛΛΑΩCΑ
ΠΟΠΗΧΩΝΔΙΑΚΟ
CΙΩΝCΥΡΟΝΤΕCΤ
ΔΙΚΤΥΟΝΤΩΝΙΧΘ
ΩΝ·ΩCΟΥΝΑΠΕ
ΒΗCΑΝΕΙCΤΗΝΓΗΝΒ
ΛΕΠΟΥCΙΝΑΝΘΡΑ
ΚΙΑΝΚΕΙΜΕΝΗΝ
ΚΑΙΟΨΑΡΙΟΝΕΠΙΚΙ
ΜΕΝΟΝΚΑΙΑΡΤ·Ν
ΛΕΓΕΙΑΥΤΟΙCΟΙC
ΕΝΕΓΚΑΤΑΙΑΠΟΤ
ΟΨΑΡΙΩΝΩΝΕΠΙ
ΑCΑΤΕΝΥΝ·
ΕΝΕΒΗΟΥΝCΙΜ·Ν
ΠΕΤΡΟCΚΑΙΕΙΛΚΥ
CΕΝΤΟΔΙΚΤΥΟΝ
ΕΙCΤΗΝΓΗΝΜΕCΤ
ΙΧΘΥΩΝΜΕΓΑΛ
ΕΚΑΤΟΝΠΕΝΤΗΚ
ΤΑΤΡΙΩΝ·ΚΑΙΤΟ
ΤΩΝΟΝΤΩΝΟΥ
ΚΕCΧΙCΘΗΤΟΔΙ
ΚΤΥΟΝ·ΛΕΓΕΙΑΥΤ
CΑΤΕΟΥΔΙCΔΕΕΤ
ΜΑΤΩΝΜΑΘΗΤ·
ΕΞΕΤΑCΑΙΑΥΤΟΝ·Τ
ΤΙCΕΙCΕΙΔΟΤΕCΟΤΙ
ΟΚCΕCΤΙΝ·ΕΡΧΕ
ΤΑΙΟΙCΚΑΙΛΑΜΒΑ
ΝΕΙΤΟΝΑΡΤΟΝΚ
ΔΙΔΩCΙΝΑΥΤΟΙC
ΩCΤΟΥΤΟΔΕΗΔΗ
ΤΡΙΤΟΝΕΦΑΝΕΡΩ
ΘΗΟΙCΤΟΙCΜΑΘ·
ΤΑΙCΕΓΕΡΘΕΙCΕΚ
ΝΕΚΡΩΝ·ΟΤΕΟΥΝ
ΗΡΙCΤΗCΑΝΛΕΓΕΙ
ΤΩCΙΜΩΝΙΠΕΤ·
ΟΙCCΙΜΩΝΑΝΝΙΩ

ΜΕΠΛΕΟΝΤΟΥΤ·
ΛΕΓΕΙΑΥΤΩΝΑΙ
ΚΕCΥΟΙΔΑCΟΤΙ
ΦΙΛΩCΕΛΕΓΕΙΑΥ
ΤΩΒΟCΚΕΤΑΑΡΝΙ
ΑΜΟΥ·ΠΑΛΙΝΛΕ
ΓΕΙΑΥΤΩCΙΜΩΝ
ΙΩΑΝΝΟΥΑΓΑΠΑ
ΜΕΛΕΓΕΙΑΥΤΩΝΑΙ
ΚΕCΥΟΙΔΑCΟΤΙ
ΦΙΛΩCΕΛΕΓΕΙΑΥ
ΤΩΠΟΙΜΑΙΝΕΤΑ
ΠΡΟΚΑΤΑΜΟΥ·Λ
ΓΕΙΑΥΤΩΤΟΤΡΙ·
CΙΜΩΝΙΩΑΝΝ·
ΦΙΛΕΙCΜΕΕΛΥΠ
ΘΗΟΠΕΤΡΟCΟ
ΤΙΕΙΠΕΝΑΥΤΩΤ·
ΤΡΙΤΟΝΚΑΙΦΙΛ·
ΜΕΚΑΙΛΕΓΕΙΑΥ
ΤΩΚΕΠΑΝΤΑCΥ
ΟΙΔΑCCΥΓΙΝΩCΚ
ΟΤΙΦΙΛΩCΕΚΑΙ
ΛΕΓΕΙΑΥΤΩΟΚCΒ
ΤΑΠΡΟΚΑΤΑΜΟΥ
ΑΜΗΝΑΜΗΝΛΕΓ
CΟΙΟΤΕΗCΝΕΩ
ΤΕΡΟCΕΖΩΝΝ
ΕCCΕΑΥΤΟΝ·ΚΑΙΠ
ΡΙΕΠΑΤΕΙCΟΠΟΥΗ
ΘΕΛΕCΟΤΑΝΔΕΓΗ
ΡΑCΗCΕΚΤΕΝΙC
ΧΙΡΑCCΟΥΚΑΙΑΛ
ΛΟΙCΩCΟΥCΙΝCΕ
ΚΑΙΠΟΙΗCΟΥCΙΝ
CΟΙΟCΟΥΘΕΛΕΙC
ΤΟΥΤΟΔΕΕΙΠΕΝ
ΜΑΙΝΩΝΠΟΙΩ
ΘΑΝΑΤΩΔΟΞΑC·
ΤΟΝΘΝ·ΚΑΙΤΟΥΤ
ΕΙΠΩΝΛΕΓΕΙ
ΤΩΑΚΟΛΟΥΘΙΜ·
ΕΠΙCΤΡΑΦΕΙCΔΕ
ΟΠΕΤΡΟCΚΑΙΕΠΙΤ
ΜΑΘΗΤΗΝΟΝΗΓΑ
ΠΑΟΙCΚΑΙΑΝΕΠ
CΕΝΕΝ ΤΩΔΙΠΝ·
ΕΠΙΤΟCΤΗΘΟCΑ·

ΤΟΥΚΑΙΛΕΓΕΙΑΥΤ·
ΚΕΤΙCΕCΤΙΝΟΠΑ
ΡΑΔΙΔΟΥCCΕΤΟΥΤ·
ΟΥΝΙΔΩΝΟΠΕΤ·
ΕΙΠΕΝΤΩΙΥΟΥΤ·
ΛΕΓΕΙΑΥΤΩ
ΟΙCΕΑΝΑΥΤΟΝΘ
ΛΩΜΕΝΙΝΕΩCΕ
ΧΟΜΑΙΤΙΠΡΟCCΕ
CΥΜΟΙΑΚΟΛΟΥΘΙ
ΕΞΗΛΘΕΝΟΥΝΟΥ
ΤΟCΟΛΟΓΟCΕΙCΤ·
ΑΔΕΛΦΟΥCΟΤΙΟ
ΜΑΘΗΤΗCΕΚΕΙ
ΝΟCΟΥΚΑΠΟΘΝΗ
CΚΕΙΟΥΚΕΙΠΕΝΔ·ΚΑ
ΑΥΤΩΟΙCΟΥΚΑ
ΠΟΘΝΗCΚΕΙΑΛΛ
ΑΝΑΥΤΟΝΘΕΛΩ
ΜΕΝΕΙΝΕΩC
ΜΑΙΟΥΤΟCΕCΤΙΝ
ΜΑΘΗΤΗCΟΜΑΡΤ
ΡΩΝΠΕΡΙΤΟΥΤΩΝ
ΚΑΙΓΡΑΨΑCΤΑΥΤΑ
ΚΑΙΟΙΔΑΜΕΝΟΤΙ
ΑΛΗΘΗCΕCΤΙΝΗ
ΜΑΡΤΥΡΙΑΑΥΤΟΥ·
ΕCΤΙΝΔΕΚΑΙΑΛΛΑ
ΠΟΛΛΑΑΕΠΟΙΗC·Ν
ΟΙCΑΤΙΝΑΕΑΝΓΡΑ
ΦΗΤΑΙΚΑΘΕΝΟΥ
ΔΑΥΤΟΝΟΙΜΑΙΤΟΝ
ΚΟCΜΟΝΧΩΡΗCΤ·
ΤΑΓΡΑΦΟΜΕΝΑΒΙ
ΚΛΙΑ:

ΕΥΑΓΓΕΛΙΟΝ
ΚΑΤΑ
ΙΩΑΝΝΗΝ

In the First Letter to the Corinthians, for example, the original scribe (A) had omitted copying several lines from the opening of Paul's famous definition of love (1 Corinthians 13:1-3). In reviewing A's text Scribe D noticed this omission, marked it, and inserted the missing text in the margin above. At the beginning of Luke's Gospel, so gross was the error committed by the original scribe (A) that Scribe D chose to replace four complete pages with four others specially copied by him.

The place of production of the Codex has been much debated. Most scholars have argued for an attribution to one of the major cities of the Mediterranean, such as Alexandria, or Caesarea in Palestine, or even Rome. Their arguments have been based on the textual character, technical sophistication and likely expense of producing the Codex. In support of an origin in Caesarea some critics have sought to identify Codex Sinaiticus as one of the fifty copies of scripture commissioned by Constantine the Great shortly after the formal dedication of Constantinople on 11 May 330 from the famous early Christian scholar Eusebius, Bishop of Caesarea. Within a letter addressed to Eusebius Constantine specified that these copies of scripture were to be written by expert scribes and easy to read. Brought to the capital by two wagons from the *Cursus Publicus*, the most privileged method of transport across the empire, they were to be distributed for use in the new churches that were being established there. Most recently, however, one scholar has not only argued against an origin in Caesarea, but also proposed that the Codex was produced in a less prominent centre. Whatever its origins, the Codex undoubtedly mirrors the growing status of the Christian Church during the 4th century and its increasing patronage and adoption by the rich and powerful. Its production, as well as that of Codex Vaticanus, also is linked to contemporary efforts to establish a definitive collection of texts that made up the Christian Bible and to clarify the specific purpose and authority of each text. Most notably in his famous Easter Letter of AD 367, Athanasius, Patriarch of Alexandria, distinguished for Christians in his patriarchate three categories of text: first, all the books of the Bible that he considered sources of faith and worthy of public reading; second, all the books regarded as inspired and worthy of private reading, particularly by those wishing to be instructed in Christian doctrine, but not of reading in public; third, all the fabrications of heretics.

The core text of the Codex produced by the 4th-century team of scribes has an individual character, encompassing texts of significantly different character and value. Whereas its text of the Gospels and Acts is highly regarded by scholars, that of Revelation is much less so. Recent research has noted significant textual differences within even such an apparently cohesive unit as the Four Gospels. Within the Gospel of John it has also revealed adjoining blocks of text of different character. It is likely that such differences reflect the different manuscripts from which the various books and parts of books were copied into Codex Sinaiticus. Behind the Codex, therefore, appears to stand a whole library of smaller books each containing different books of the Bible. In this sense Codex Sinaiticus is the quintessential Bible, faithfully mirroring the plurality of the Greek words 'ta biblia' ('the books') from which our English word 'Bible' derives.

Between the 5th and 7th centuries, well after the original production of the Codex, the character of its text was significantly altered. In a second important wave of corrections a scholar now known as corrector C^a not only amended errors made by the original scribes and not subsequently revised, but also attempted to bring the entire text into line with a version that was more familiar to him. In doing so he sometimes revived the version copied by the original scribe and reversed earlier corrections made during the production of the manuscript. In Luke's description of the Crucifixion, for example, C^a restored the passage 'Then said Jesus, "Father, forgive them; for they know not what they do"'. Another corrector, known as $C^{Pamph.}$, is renowned for two inscriptions that he added at the end of 2 Esdras (Nehemiah) and Esther in the Leipzig portion of the Codex. According to these inscriptions, the corrections that he made to the text from 1 Samuel to Esther were based on another manuscript containing only these texts, which had itself been checked against probably the most famous lost Biblical manuscript of the early Christian period, the *Hexapla* of the great Alexandrian scholar Origen. Within the intermediary manuscript was apparently written:
'*Compared and corrected against the* Hexapla *of Origen... The confessor Antoninus checked it. Pamphilus corrected the book in prison, through God's great grace and magnanimity*'.
Since this major edition of the Old Testament in six parallel Hebrew and Greek versions was completed by Origen at Caesarea and since the intermediary manuscript containing 1 Samuel to Esther was almost

Codex Sinaiticus. Conclusion of Esther and beginning of Tobit. In the second column is one of the two inscriptions relating to Pamphilus and Antoninus. Leipzig, Universitätsbibliothek, MS gr. 1, f. 19

ΕΙΡΩΘΕΝΚΩΠΟΛΛΑ
ΩΝΑΥΤΟΥΚΑΙΕΝ
ΗΒΑΤΟΚΟΙΜΑΘΕΚ
ΠΑΝΤΩΝΤΩΝΚΑ
ΚΩΝΤΟΥΤΩΝΚΑΙ
ΕΠΟΙΗΣΕΝΟΘΕΟΟ
ΕΛΕΗΜΑΚΑΓΑΤΑ
ΒΑΤΑΤΑΜΕΓΑΛΑΩ
ΙΕΓΟΜΕΝΕΝΤΟΙΟ
ΕΘΝΕΟΙΝΚΑΤΑΤΟΥ
ΤΟΕΓΩΝΕΤΕΚΝΩΝ
ΡΟΥΟΛΥΘΕΝΑΤΟΥ
ΘΩΤΟΥΩΥΚΑΙ
ΝΑΠΑΟΙΤΟΜΕΩ
ΟΙΝΚΑΙΑΡΘΩΘΥΤΙ
ΕΙΟΘΡΑΜΙΚΝΙΕΝ
ΤΕΡΩΜΑΤΩΝΕΝΤΕ
ΚΡΙΟΕΟΘΕΟΝΙΚΑΙ
ΟΝΤΟΥΝΚΑΙΠΑ
ΤΟΟΟΤΗΘΟΙΝΚΑΙ
ΕΤΙΜΗΟΘΝΟΘΟΝ
ΛΑΟΝΑΥΤΟΥΘΑΙΕ
ΔΙΘΔΙΟΘΕΝΤΗΝ
ΚΛΗΡΟΝΟΜΙΑΝΑΝ
ΤΟΥΚΑΙΕΟΝΤΩ
ΤΟΙΟΟΥΜΕΡΑΙΩ
ΤΗΤΕΓΟΡΕΟΛΕ
ΚΑΙΤΟΥΟΥΤΟΥΙΙ
ΜΟΘΙΜΕΤΑΟΥΝΔ
ΤΟΙΟΚΑΙΧΑΡΑΟΚΑ
ΑΥΤΟΟΥΝΕΜΙ
ΤΙΟΝΤΟΥΘΥΚΑΙ
ΓΕΝΕΜΕΝΟΙΤΟΒΑΤ
ΕΝΑΕΝΤΟΛΑΙΟ
ΑΥΤΟΥΚΑΙΕΝΤΩ
ΤΑΞΕΙΕΚΟΝΤΩ
ΘΟΟΥΠΑΝΕΝΩΝ
ΚΑΙΚΑΘΩΤΙΠΡΟΟ
ΕΠΙΜΕΛΟΝΔΟΘ
ΕΙΟΘΟΘΟΝΘΝΩΙ
ΚΑΙΠΤΟΛΕΜΑΟΩ
ΟΠΟΟΟΥΤΟΥΤΗΝ
ΠΡΟΚΕΙΜΕΝΗΝ
ΘΘΤΟΛΜΗΤΩΝ
ΡΟΥΥΜΗΝΕΦΑ

ΕΙΝΑΙΚΑΙΕΡΜΗΝΙ
ΚΕΝΑΙΛΥΟΙΜΑΧ·Ν
ΠΤΟΛΕΜΑΙΟΥΤΩ
ΕΝΙΕΡΟΥΟΑΛΗΜ

ΕΟΟΝΙ

ΕΒΛΑΟΘΟΜΟΡΩΝΤΩ
ΙΕΙΟΤΟΥΤΩΘΗΝΑΙ
ΤΟΥΛΝΑΝΤΙΑΤΟΥ
ΛΑΟΥΝΑΤΟΥΤΩΒΑ
ΤΟΥΤΩΡΑΧΛΗΤΟΥΘ
ΤΟΥΝΑΕΚΠΤΥΟΙΓ
ΜΑΤΟΟΚΕΜΑΧΟΤΩΝ
ΟΟΗΚΕΜΑΧΟΤΩΝ
ΕΚΡΞΟΒΟΗΝΕΝΑΙ
ΝΕΘΕΘΕΝΟΘΤΩΝ
ΤΗΝΩΝΙΚΘΝΕΝΑΙ
ΤΘΕΝΩΝΙΚΘΝΕΝΑΙ
ΚΥΜΟΘΕΙΝΙΝ·ΤΑ
ΙΑΝΘΑΛΩΘΕΤΕΡΑΟ
ΛΕΘΡΟΝΙΘΛΑΘΟ
ΤΟΥΤΑΕΤΙΕΝΤΟΙΟ
ΤΟΥΤΑΕΝΤΟΙΟ
ΩΧΛΟΘΟΥΚΕΤΟΝ
ΩΝΙΘΩΙΚΑΙΕΧΛΛΙ
ΤΕΘΝΤΟΝ·ΚΑΤΤΟΙ
ΤΩΘΝΑΤΟΥΚΑΙΘ
ΛΕΩΝΙΕΜΟΝ·Υ
ΤΩΝΤΩΝΟΜΥΓΩ
ΝΟΙΘΤΟΕΙΟΤΩΟΥ
ΚΑΤΤΟΕΟΘΝΑΤΤ
ΝΟΤΤΟΤΟΕΟΘΝΙΑ
ΝΕΘΘΤΙΝΟΘ
ΝΘΕΘΕΚΤΙΝΟΘ
ΩΜΘΕΘΕΚΤΙΝΟΘ
ΝΕΜΕΠΘΥΚΑΙ
ΤΕΜΘΘΟΥΘΘΕΘΙΑ
ΤΩΜΟΥΘΘΟΥΘΘΕ
ΚΑΙΠΘΘΘΕΝΚΤΘ
ΝΕΘΘΝΝΚΘΝΤΟΥ
ΙΑΤΡΟΘΟΝΟΥΜΕ
ΙΤΘΘΝΝΟΥΜΕ
ΟΙΚΟΥΛΑΟΘΙΑΙΟΥ
ΙΝΤΟΘΘΘΘΙΟΥΚΝΑΙ
ΠΟΙΕΡΟΥΘΑΛΗΜΘ
ΤΟΝΟΝΤΩΘΩΝΙ
ΘΙΘΘΘΘΕΙΘΘΛΕ

ΠΑΡΑΚΙΩΦΥΛΑΘΕΙ
ΚΑΙΤΗΘΘΘΕΝΟΘΤΘ
ΟΟΤΙΘΘΘΟΧΙΝΟΙΘΝ
ΝΘΘΘΘΟΘΤΘΟΥΟΥ
ΚΑΙΟΚΟΝΟΜΘΘΘΙ
ΕΝΑΥΤΟΘΘΕΤΘΘΑΟ
ΤΘΘΘΘΟΘΘΘΘΘΘΙ
ΟΝΘΘΘΝΑΝΙΚΘΟΘ
ΘΘΘΕΘΘΘΟΘΘΘΘΘΘ
ΘΟΥΜΑΤΤΟΥΜΟΝΘ
ΘΘΘΘΘΙΜΕΝΟΟΑΤΩ
ΟΙΤΟΘΘΘΘΘΘΘΕΘ
ΑΝΘΘΘΘΘΟΥΘΘΝ
ΘΘΘΘΘΝΤΘΘΘΘΘ
ΙΘΘΙΝΘΘΘΝΘΘΝ
ΘΘΘΝΤΘΘΘΝΘΘ
ΘΘΘΝΤΘΝΘΘΘΘΘΘ
ΘΘΘΘΝΝΤΘΘΘΘΘ
ΘΘΘΘΘΝΘΘΘΘΘΘ
ΘΘΘΝΘΘΘΘΘΘΘΘ
ΕΝΤΩΝΘΘΘΘΘΝ
ΝΠΡΟΟΤΑΓΜΑΤΙΝΩ
ΝΚΟΠΤΑΟΘΘΘΘΘ
ΙΟΤΘΝΑΘΘΘΤΘΘΝΙ
ΝΚΑΙΚΑΤΑΟΘΘΘΘΙ
ΝΩΝΚΑΙΤΑΘΘΘΘ
ΤΟΚΟΥΘΘΘΘΘΘΘ
ΘΘΝΘΘΘΘΘΘΘΘ
ΠΡΘΘΝΘΘΘΘΘΘ
ΘΘΝΥΜΘΘΘΘΘΘ
ΛΥΤΘΝΤΘΘΘΘΘΘΘ
ΙΟΤΑΘΘΘΘΘΝΝΙΝ
ΠΡΟΟΤΟΝΘΘΘΘΘΝ
ΝΝΝΘΘΘΘΘΘΘΘΘΘ
ΘΘΘΘΘΘΘΘΘΘΘΘ
ΤΩΝΝΟΥΘΘΘΘΘΙΝ
ΘΘΘΝΘΘΘΘΘΝΘ
ΝΝΘΘΘΘΘΘΘΘΘΘ
ΝΘΘΘΝΝΘΘΝΘΘΘ
ΘΘΝΘΘΘΘΘΘΘΘΝΘ
ΕΙΝΘΘΘΘΘΘΘΘΘ
ΘΘΘΘΘΘΝΘΘΘΘΝ
ΘΘΘΘΘΘΘΘΘΝ
ΝΘΘΘΘΘΘΘΘΝΘΝ

certainly corrected by the early Christian martyrs Pamphilus (d. 310) and Antoninus (d. 311) in the same city, it seems probable that the Codex was in Palestine sometime between the 5th and 7th centuries.

What happened to the Codex during the following thousand years is far from certain. Although Caesarea was occupied by the Persians from AD 604 to 628, a significant Christian revival subsequently took place under the Emperor Heraclius. (Around the same time Heraclius famously recovered the Cross removed from Jerusalem by the Persian invaders.) By AD 642, however, the city had fallen to the Arabs, and, despite its recovery by the Crusaders in the 12th century, Caesarea ceased to be an important Christian centre. From the manuscript itself we learn that it continued to be consulted and its text occasionally corrected by readers. Several annotations in Arabic confirm that it remained in the Middle East, and others in Greek bearing the names of particular monks provide clear evidence of its presence in a Greek-speaking Christian monastery. Given the significant cultural changes that occurred in the Middle East during these thousand years, this second observation appears to confirm the tradition that the Codex found a home during this period in the Sinai desert at the Orthodox Monastery of St Catherine.

After this period the Codex begins to emerge from the mists of time. In 1761 the Italian naturalist Vitaliano Donati reported having seen at the Monastery of St Catherine 'a Bible comprising leaves of handsome, large, delicate and square-shaped parchment, written in a round and handsome script'. Most spectacularly, however, it was here that in 1844 the monks brought to the attention of the German biblical scholar Constantine Tischendorf a substantial portion of what he immediately recognised as a hugely significant early copy of the Bible. Driven by an overwhelming desire to underpin the authority of the Christian scriptures by means of indisputable physical evidence and to reassert to contemporary sceptical rationalism their antiquity and reliability, Tischendorf had committed himself to the search for ancient manuscripts of the Bible. Now, in 1844, on his first tour of the Middle East, he found himself in the fortunate position of having discovered exactly what he wanted. Shortly afterwards he was able to take 43 leaves of the manuscript that he had seen at St Catherine's back to Leipzig and to secure them for his home University. Since its publication by Tischendorf in 1846 this portion of the Codex has been known as the Codex Friderico-Augustanus, named in honour of the editor's patron, King Frederick Augustus II of Saxony.

Tischendorf's first visit to St Catherine's was to prove a mere prelude to more famous later events. For, although a second visit in 1853 brought to light only one further fragment of the Codex, a third visit in 1859 resulted in the greatest discovery of his career. In his own words:

'I knew that I held in my hand the most precious Biblical treasure in existence – a document whose age and importance exceeded that of all the manuscripts which I had ever examined during twenty years' study of the subject. I cannot now, I confess, recall all the emotions which I felt in that exciting moment with such a diamond in my possession. Though my lamp was dim, and the night cold, I sat down at once to transcribe the Epistle of Barnabas.'

Tischendorf was particularly quick in recognising the importance of the 135 leaves bearing the complete text of the New Testament, as well as the seven with the Epistle of Barnabas. To allow him more time to transcribe this text and that of the Old Testament, he requested permission for the temporary removal of all 347 leaves of the Codex from the monastery to Cairo. However, before the end of 1859 Tischendorf was in St Petersburg, and on 19 November he presented his entire find to the sponsor of his third expedition to Sinai, Tsar Alexander II of Russia. Three years later, in 1862, Tischendorf published a lavish edition of the complete text that is a lasting testament to his extraordinary abilities as a textual scholar. Although Tischendorf's right to make this donation was almost immediately challenged, a transfer of ownership from the monastery to the Russian state was formalised in 1869 after lengthy negotiations led by the Imperial Ministry of Foreign Affairs. At this point the 347 leaves were moved to the Imperial Public Library in St Petersburg, where they immediately became one of its greatest treasures.

Yet, the travels of the Codex did not end there. By the summer of 1933 it had become known in Britain that the Soviet government of Joseph Stalin wished to raise desperately needed foreign capital by selling the Codex through the London booksellers Maggs. Championed by the Prime Minister Ramsay MacDonald, Archbishop of Canterbury Cosmo Lang, and biblical scholar and former Director of the British Museum, Sir Frederic Kenyon, a national campaign to raise the necessary funds was soon underway. Although American interest in the Codex was tempered by the Depression, time remained of essence. In line with the aims of MacDonald's National Government rich and poor alike were encouraged to combine their monetary resources in contributions ranging from a half-farthing to several hundred pounds, thereby securing full payment of the then huge agreed price of £100,000 sterling. Indeed

Red tin box in which
Codex Sinaiticus was
stored in the Imperial
Public Library at St
Petersburg. British
Library, Add. MS 43725

so successful was the public subscription campaign that in the end the British Government expended significantly less than the £50,000 that it had been prepared to commit to the purchase. Against a backdrop of intense public interest and media coverage the Codex arrived at the British Museum two days after Christmas on 27 December 1933, accompanied by Maurice Ettinghausen from Maggs, two detectives from Vine Street Police Station, and a reporter from the *Daily Express*. After a formal handover and checking of its contents, the Codex went on public display in the front hall of the British Museum. Day after day the queue of visitors stretched out into the Museum forecourt, as people of all classes waited patiently to get sight of the famous Codex which many felt had been narrowly saved from destruction by an atheistic Soviet regime.

The largest portion of Codex Sinaiticus is now one of the greatest treasures of the British Library. Together with the rest of the manuscripts and books that had formed the British Museum Library, the Codex was transferred to the newly established British Library in 1973. It has been on permanent display ever since its arrival in London and can currently be seen in the Library's John Ritblat Gallery. Just as its presence in Russia enabled a collotype facsimile to be produced between 1911 and 1922, its coming to Britain stimulated the publication of a landmark reappraisal of the Codex in 1938. Subsequent scholarly research on the Codex has generated an immense literature.

Handover of Codex Sinaiticus at the British Museum, 27 December 1933. Those present include Ernest Maggs (left), Sir Frederic Kenyon (centre), and Sir George Hill (right). British Library, Add. MS 68923, f. 1

INFRA-RED RAY ON £100,000 BIBLE

WILL IT REVEAL CENTURIES-OLD SECRETS?

5,000 FORM QUEUES TO SEE MANUSCRIPT

SPECIAL GUARD

By A Special Correspondent

THE £100,000 fourth-century Bible manuscript Codex Sinaiticus, bought from the Soviet Government, was yesterday handed over to the British Museum authorities and lodged in the Museum, where it will remain the property of the nation for all time.

It is one of the oldest Bible manuscripts known to man, being originally written about 340 A.D. Later additions were made to it, and it now consists of 346 leaves of fine vellum about 15in. by 13½in. written in beautiful Greek characters. Sir George Hill, director of the British Museum, Sir Frederic Kenyon, the leading expert on Bible manuscripts, and other authorities spent several hours yesterday examining the manuscript at the Museum.

Later it was placed in a special case in the entrance hall, and by the time the museum closed at 8 p.m. more than 5,000 people, who had formed in long queues, had seen it.

Almost every one of them put money in the collecting-box by the side of the case.

This box has been placed there to receive contributions towards the £50,000

The £100,000 Bible, wrapped in brown paper, leaving Bush House for the British Museum.

which it is hoped will be raised by public subscription. The remaining £50,000 of the purchase price has been guaranteed by the Government.

Romance of Discovery

Among those who came to see the Codex was Mr. Walter Tischendorf. He is a grandson of Dr. Tischendorf, who in 1844 found the manuscript in a monastery on Mount Sinai—a discovery which was one of the great romances of Biblical research.

The drama of the discovery of the Codex has been many times told, and Mr. Ernest Maggs, the London bookseller, has also told of his two-years negotiation with the Soviet Government for its purchase.

Yet its arrival and delivery yesterday were marked with nothing more than the prosaic procedure customary in commonplace business transactions.

Simple Receipt

It was handed over to Mr. Maggs and his partner, Dr. Ettinghausen, at the offices of Arcos, Ltd., in Bush House, Aldwych, and they signed a receipt which read:

"One Greek MS. received from Arcos, Ltd., the 'Codex Sinaiticus,' on behalf of Maggs Bros., acting for the British Museum Trustees, as arranged by our letters to you."

The Codex was then taken to Conduit-street, W., where in the more fitting setting of Mr. Maggs's rooms it was unpacked.

There, in a mass of cottonwool, the treasured manuscript lay, naked of

any binding, on an oak table. Its Greek characters stood out boldly on vellum mellowed with the passage of centuries.

Looking at it and turning its pages, there came to me a sense of being indescribably puny and awed.

Soon they took the manuscript away—wrapped in brown paper—to the Museum, where a special guard has been placed over it in addition to the patrols who are always present to protect the treasures in the great building.

Mr. Maggs was at first asked £500,000 by the Soviet authorities for the Codex, but after two years of negotiation secured it for £100,000.

Hidden Room

Sir Frederic Kenyon represented the British Museum Trustees in the purchase negotiations. He and Mr. Maggs, acting as intermediary for the Soviet, held their conferences in a hidden room at Mr. Maggs's Conduit-street premises.

This room, containing historical treasures worth a fortune, is a replica of a 15th-century monks' study. Its oak panelling is in the exact tradition, and even the heavy nails in the doors and the iron lamps were beaten out by hand.

With the coming of the "Codex" to the British Museum begins an intensive study of it in which infra-red rays will be used to wrest from the many faded and hitherto undecipherable sections secrets that it has held down the centuries.

What this examination will reveal is a matter of the most profound interest to Christianity.

Mr. Maggs told a "Daily Mail" reporter yesterday that it is possible that the context of whole phrases attributed to Christ may be altered by what modern science in the form of infra-red rays will show.

FILM'S BIG SUCCESS

DEMAND EVERYWHERE FOR "ALICE IN WONDERLAND"

By SETON MARGRAVE, Our Film Correspondent

"Alice in Wonderland" has been such an outstanding success that the thirteen copies of the film now in Britain will be in constant use until the end of January, after which it is proposed to withdraw the film from circulation, while preparing for the general release of approximately 120 copies next Christmas.

In spite of being on view at seven other cinemas in London, "Alice" has been so successful at the Plaza, Piccadilly-circus, that it will be retained for matinees next week, although the policy of the Plaza is to change its films every week.

The difficulty is that there is only a limited number of copies of the film in the country. Besides being the most appropriate talking picture of the season, "Alice" has therefore acquired a rarity value, and has created the unprecedented situation of being in demand everywhere.

Prints, however, cannot be supplied, because no negative has yet arrived in London from Hollywood.

NURSE'S LOVE TRAGEDY

A nurse's tragic love for a married man who died recently was revealed at the inquest at Paddington yesterday on Edith Dawn Beresford, aged 32, who was found gassed in bed at her address in Elgin-avenue, Maida Vale, W., on Christmas Eve.

Her father, Mr. William Beresford, of St. Ives-road, Blacktown, said that his daughter was in love with a man who, it was discovered, was married and who died in May. She was very upset by his death.

Mr. Ingleby Oddie, in recording a verdict of Suicide while of Unsound Mind, mentioned that Miss Beresford had left "a whole lot of letters, all

RUSH TO SEE THE £100,000 BIBLE.—A scene in the British Museum after the fourth century Bible manuscript Codex Sinaiticus, bought from the Soviet Government, had been placed in the entrance hall. More than 5,000 people inspected it.

HANDING OVER THE £100,000 BIBLE

The Codex Sinaiticus, bought from the Soviet Government for £100,000, being handed over to Mr. E. Maggs, who negotiated the purchase, at Bush House yesterday. Inset: A section of the 1,600-years-old manuscript, which now (as reported in Page 7) reposes in the British Museum.

THE CODEX SINAITICUS

OR

MOUNT SINAI BIBLE

probably the second in date of the three great early manuscripts of the Greek Bible, the first being the Codex Vaticanus, in the library of the Vatican, and the third the Codex Alexandrinus, in the British Museum; written by at least three scribes in uncial characters on fine vellum and corrected by several hands at various periods. The MS., written in the fourth century, perhaps in the same place as the Codex Vaticanus and very likely in Egypt, was found by Tischendorf in the monastery of St. Catherine on Mount Sinai in 1844 and 1859. Forty-three leaves, from the Old Testament, found in 1844, were presented by him to the King of Saxony, and are now at Leipzig; the remainder, 347 leaves in all, comprising extensive parts of the Old Testament and all the New Testament, with the Epistle of Barnabas and the Shepherd of Hermas, found in 1859, were presented to Alexander II of Russia, and are here exhibited. Other Bible Manuscripts of interest, and a view of the monastery about the time of the discovery, are in adjoining cases.

Subscriptions, large or small, are earnestly solicited, and may be sent to the Director or to the Hon. Secretary, Friends of the National Libraries, British Museum. Small sums may also be placed in the box adjoining this case; and promises of future subscriptions may be written in the book provided for the purpose.

ΗΝ ΟΙ ΓΕΝΗ ΚΑΙ ΤΑΣ ΓΡΑΦΑС
ΚΑΙ ΑΝΑСΤΑΝΤΕΣ ΑΥΤΗ ΤΗ ΩΡΑ
ΥΠΕСΤΡΕΨΑΝ ΕΙС ΙΛΗΜ ΚΑΙ ΕΥ
ΡΟΝ СΥΝΗΘΡΟΙСΜΕΝΟΥС ΤΟΥС
ΕΝΔΕΚΑ ΚΑΙ ΤΟΥС СΥΝ ΑΥΤΟΙС
ΛΕΓΟΝΤΑС ΟΤΙ ΗΓΕΡΘΗ Ο ΚС ΟΝ
ΤΩС ΚΑΙ ΩΦΘΗ СΙΜΩΝΙ ΚΑΙ
ΑΥΤΟΙ ΕΞΗΓΟΥΝΤΟ ΤΑ ΕΝ ΤΗ ΟΔΩ
ΚΑΙ ΩС ΕΓΝΩСΘΗ ΑΥΤΟΙС ΕΝ
ΤΗ ΚΛΑСΕΙ ΤΟΥ ΑΡΤΟΥ
ΤΑΥΤΑ ΔΕ ΑΥΤΩΝ ΛΑΛΟΥΝΤΩΝ
ΑΥΤΟС ΟС ΕСΤΗ ΕΝ ΜΕСΩ ΑΥ
ΤΩΝ ΚΑΙ ΛΕΓΕΙ ΑΥΤΟΙС ΕΙΡΗΝΗ
ΥΜΙΝ ΤΤΟΗΘΕΝΤΕС ΔΕ ΚΑΙ
ΕΜΦΟΒΟΙ ΓΕΝΟΜΕΝΟΙ ΕΔΟ
ΚΟΥΝ ΠΝΑ ΘΕΩΡΕΙΝ ΚΑΙ ΕΙΠΕΝ
ΑΥΤΟΙС ΤΙ ΤΕΤΑΡΑΓΜΕΝΟΙ Ε
СΤΑΙ ΓΕ ΚΑΙ ΔΙΑ ΤΙ ΔΙΑΛΟΓΙСΜΟΙ
ΑΝΑΒΑΙΝΟΥСΙΝ ΕΝ ΤΑΙС ΚΑΡ
ΔΙΑΙС ΥΜΩΝ ΙΔΕΤΕ ΤΑС ΧΕΙ
ΡΑС ΜΟΥ ΚΑΙ ΤΟΥС ΠΟΔΑС ΜΟΥ
ΟΤΙ ΑΥΤΟС ΕΓΩ ΕΙΜΙ ΨΗΛΑΦΗ
СΑΤΕ ΜΕ ΚΑΙ ΙΔΕΤΕ ΟΤΙ ΠΝΑ
СΑΡΚΑ ΚΑΙ ΟСΤΕΑ ΟΥΚ ΕΧΕΙ
ΚΑΘΩС ΕΜΕ ΘΕΩΡΕΙΤΕ ΕΧΟΝΤΑ
ΚΑΙ ΤΟΥΤΟ ΕΙΠΩΝ ΕΠΕΔΕΙΞΕ
ΑΥΤΟΙС ΤΑС ΧΕΙΡΑС ΚΑΙ ΤΟΥС
ΠΟΔΑС   ΕΤΙ ΔΕ ΑΠΙСΤΟΥΝ
ΤΩΝ ΑΥΤΩΝ ΚΑΙ ΘΑΥΜΑΖΟΝΤΩ
ΧΑΡΑС ΕΙΠΕΝ ΑΥΤΟΙС
ΕΧΕΤΕ ΤΙ ΒΡΩСΙΜΟΝ ΕΝΘΑΔΕ
ΟΙ ΔΕ ΕΠΕΔΩΚΑΝ ΑΥΤΩ ΙΧΘΥΟС
ΟΠΤΟΥ ΜΕΡΟС ΚΑΙ ΛΑΒΩΝ
ΕΝΩΠΙΟΝ ΑΥΤΩΝ ΕΦΑΓΕ
ΕΙΠΕΝ ΔΕ ΑΥΤΟΙС ΟΥΤΟΙ ΟΙ ΛΟΓΟΙ
ΜΟΥ ΟΥС ΕΛΑΛΗСΑ ΠΡΟС ΥΜΑС
ΕΤΙ ΩΝ СΥΝ ΥΜΙΝ ΟΤΙ ΔΕΙ
ΠΛΗΡΩΘΗΝΑΙ ΠΑΝΤΑ ΤΑ ΓΕ
ΓΡΑΜΜΕΝΑ ΕΝ ΤΩ ΝΟΜΩ
ΜΩСΕΩС ΚΑΙ ΠΡΟΦΗΤΑΙС
ΚΑΙ ΨΑΛΜΟΙС ΠΕΡΙ ΕΜΟΥ
ΤΟΤΕ ΔΙΗΝΟΙΞΕΝ ΑΥΤΩΝ ΤΟ
ΝΟΥΝ ΤΟΥ СΥΝΙΕΝΑΙ ΤΑС ΓΡΑ
ΦΑС ΚΑΙ ΕΙΠΕΝ ΑΥΤΟΙС ΟΤΙ
ΟΥΤΩС ΓΕΓΡΑΠΤΑΙ ΚΑΙ ΟΥ
ΤΩС ΕΔΕΙ ΠΑΘΕΙΝ ΤΟΝ ΧΝ
ΚΑΙ ΑΝΑСΤΗΝΑΙ ΕΚ ΝΕΚΡΩ
ΤΗ ΤΡΙΤΗ ΗΜΕΡΑ ΚΑΙ ΚΗΡΥ
ΧΘΗΝΑΙ ΕΠΙ ΤΩ ΟΝΟΜΑΤΙ ΑΥ
ΤΟΥ ΜΕΤΑΝΟΙΑΝ ΚΑΙ ΑΦΕ
СΙΝ ΑΜΑΡΤΙΩΝ ΕΙС ΠΑΝΤΑ

ΤΑ ΕΘΝΗ ΑΡΞΑΜΕΝΟΝ ΑΠ
ΡΙΗΜ ΥΜΕΙС ΔΕ ΕСΤΑΙ ΜΑ
ΡΕС ΤΟΥΤΩΝ ΚΑΙ ΑΔΟΥ Ε
ΑΠΟСΤΕΛΛΩ ΤΗΝ ΕΠΑΓΓ
ΤΟΥ ΠΡС ΜΟΥ ΕΦ ΥΜΑС ΥΜ
ΔΕ ΚΑΘΙСΑΤΕ ΕΝ ΤΗ ΠΟΛ
ΕΩС ΟΥ ΕΝΔΥСΗСΘΑΙ ΔΥ
ΜΙΝ ΕΞ ΥΨΟΥС ΕΞΗΓΑΓΕ
ΑΥΤΟΥС ΕΞΩ ΕΩС ΕΙС ΒΗ
ΚΑΙ ΕΠΑΡΑС ΤΑС ΧΕΙΡΑС Α
ΕΥΛΟΓΗСΕΝ ΑΥΤΟΥС
ΚΑΙ ΕΓΕΝΕΤΟ ΕΝ ΤΩ ΕΥΛ
ΑΥΤΟΝ ΑΥΤΟΥС ΔΙΕСΤΗ
ΤΩ ΚΑΙ ΑΝΕΦΕΡΕΤΟ ΕΙС Τ
ΟΥΝΟΝ ΚΑΙ ΑΥΤΟΙ ΠΡΟС
СΑΝΤΕС ΑΥΤΟΝ ΥΠΕСΤ
ΕΙС ΙΛΗΜ ΜΕΤΑ ΧΑΡΑС ΜΕ
ΚΑΙ ΗСΑΝ ΔΙΑ ΠΑΝΤΟС ΕΝ
ΤΕС ΚΑΙ ΕΥΛΟΓΟΥΝΤΕС
ΟΝ ΑΜΗΝ

СΥΝ ΤΩ ΙΩΑΝΝΗ ΚΑΤΑ ΛΟΥΚ

CODEX SINAITICUS & CODEX ALEXANDRINUS

Together with Codex Vaticanus, Codex Sinaiticus stands at the head of parchment *codices* of the Greek Bible. Closely following is another remarkable survivor from the early Christian period. Comprising 773 parchment leaves and now divided into four volumes, Codex Alexandrinus contains the whole of the Greek Old and New Testaments and Apocrypha. It preserves one of the best texts of Deuteronomy and Revelation, and is the oldest manuscript of the second and third books of Maccabees. It concludes with two letters to the Christian community at Corinth ascribed to Clement of Rome. Generally dated to the 5th century and written, like Codex Sinaiticus, in a fine majuscule (upper case) script, Alexandrinus constitutes another landmark in the history of the Bible and the book.

Codex Alexandrinus is named after the capital of Greek Egypt, Alexandria. It is not, however, an ancient heirloom of the patriarchs of Alexandria. The earliest date at which it was known to have been in Alexandria is around the beginning of the 14th century. At this point the patriarch Athanasius II destined it for the patriarchal Monastery of St Saba in Alexandria. Athanasius had spent most of his active life embroiled in ecclesiastical politics at Constantinople and all the other manuscripts that he collected and destined for the patriarchate were acquired far from Alexandria. By Athanasius's time Alexandria was not the city that it had once been. As a result of the Monophysite schism in the middle of the 5th century the Orthodox patriarch of Alexandria had ceased to be the Christian spiritual leader in Egypt. In 642 the city had

Codex Alexandrinus. Conclusion of the Gospel of Luke. British Library, Royal MS 1 D viii, f. 65v fallen to the Arab general 'Amr Ibn al 'Asi, and, although Alexandria's prosperity continued, serious decline began in the 8th and 9th centuries. The once famous Greek Catechetical School headed by Clement and Origen had disappeared. With it had disappeared its presumed extensive library, the Christian successor to the pagan Great Library of Alexandria.

In 1627 the then Orthodox patriarch of Constantinople, Cyril Lucar, presented Codex Alexandrinus to King Charles I as a New Year's gift. Since then Codex Alexandrinus has rightly been treasured in Britain. Although it arrived in England too late to be used for the Authorised Version of the Bible (1611), the Codex stimulated further study of the text of the New Testament and thus underpins all subsequent editions and translations. Formerly the jewel of the English royal library, Alexandrinus has survived all threats of alienation and destruction to join Codex Sinaiticus as one of the greatest treasures of the British Library.

Comparison of these two early codices of the Greek Bible held by the British Library is instructive and reasserts their individuality. It also illustrates very well how far the early Christian book had developed by the 5th century and how much of what became the standard language of medieval manuscripts and early printed books was formed during late antiquity. Most obviously the makers of Alexandrinus established a smaller format for its pages. They also reduced the number of columns of text from four to two to the page, and in so doing substantially increased the width of each column. They undertook seriously the task of articulating and managing its text by the introduction of enlarged letters and titling in red ink. Whereas in Sinaiticus a new paragraph is highlighted by slightly extending the first letter of a line into the left margin, in Alexandrinus a new paragraph is highlighted by enlarging that letter and setting it clearly apart in the margin. The scribes of Sinaiticus always began a new paragraph on a new line. The scribes of Alexandrinus sometimes merely left a small space between the end of one and the beginning of the next and enlarged the first letter of the next line. The latter practice became the standard one for Greek scribes.

Whereas Sinaiticus has titling in red only in the Psalms and the Song of Solomon, Alexandrinus has red ink in many more portions of text, including the first line or lines of each Book and all the text of the tables of chapter headings at the beginning of each Gospel. The makers of Alexandrinus also elaborated the titles that appear at the end of each of its books of the Bible into true book decoration. Here they incorporated stylised versions of early Christian symbols and executed part of the decoration in red ink. The contrast with the much simpler end-titles of Sinaiticus is very telling. Had the canon tables of Alexandrinus survived, these would almost certainly have offered us the earliest surviving decorated example of this significant accompaniment to the Gospels. In them we may have had the antecedents of the splendid Golden Canon Tables from the 6th century, also preserved in the British Library, and of the many subsequent versions of Eusebius's tables in which manuscript illuminators lavished so much of their art.

ΚΑΝΟΝωΝ ΘΙΟΥΚΑΝΑΤΤΥ ΔΕ ΘΙΤΙ
ΘΥΑΓΓΘΛΙΟΤω ΜΟΙΤΟΙΟΝΔΗΤΕΘΙΘ ΘΑ
ΟΤΗΘΑΙΤΙΝΙωθΟΥΔΘΙΚΘ ΔΛΛΑΙ
ΝΘΟΤΑΓΓΑΡΑΓΓΑΠΘΙΑΘΙ ΜΙΑΘ
ΟΥΘΘΚΑΟΤΟΥ ΤΟΓΓΘΥΘΘΥΙΘΙ
ΛΥΤΓωΝΗΜΘΧΟΙΟΛΗΝΘΘΤΑΧΙΘ
ΑΜΑΛΛΑΒΟΝΤΘΤΓΓΡΟΚΘΙΜΘΝΘ
ΖΗΤΗΘΘΑΘΘΘΛΥΓΓΟΝΘΝΤΟΙΘΚ
ΚΝΙΧΘΑΡΘΦΘΟΥΤΓΘΘΗΜΙωΝ
ΘΙΘΙΜΘΝΘΝΘΥΟΥΘΘΚΤωΝΘΝΤΙ
ΚΑΝΟΝΟΘΘΓΓΡΟΓΡΑΦωΝΓΙΘΘ
ΓΓΘΡΙΟΥΖΗΤΗΘΘΙΘ ΘΙ ΡΗΚΑΘ ω
ΚΑΝΤΘΙΘ Χω ΝΟΓΓωΝΘΟΤ

CODEX SINAITICUS AND BYZANTINE
MANUSCRIPTS OF THE BIBLE

Within the eastern half of the former Roman Empire, including its capital Constantinople – or Byzantium – the Christian scriptures in Greek came to be copied many thousands of times. According to the authoritative list maintained by the Institute for New Testament Studies at Münster, there are 5746 surviving manuscripts of parts of the New Testament in Greek, including 118 papyri. Of these manuscripts only 60 include the whole New Testament. Even if manuscripts that exclude Revelation, the status of which was at best uncertain within the Eastern Church, are included in the figure of complete New Testaments, the number rises to only 207, or around 3.5% of the total surviving manuscripts. Restricting the field to those manuscripts produced before the 11th century, only six contain the complete New Testament and a further three include everything apart from Revelation. These nine manuscripts form just over 0.15% of the total 5746.

Out of all the manuscripts produced between the early Christian period and the 16th century, manuscripts that embrace both Old and New Testaments in Greek are even rarer. These total no more than twelve, seven of which date from before the 11th century and four from the 4th and 5th centuries. Although extremely vulnerable as vast quarries of parchment that could be re-used for the production of later manuscripts, whole Bibles in Greek were probably as rare relative to contemporary manuscripts of parts of the Bible as the figures based on surviving manuscripts suggest. Thus, there appears to have been no continuing

The Golden Canon Tables, made at Constantinople in the 6th or 7th century. The preface of Eusebius of Caesarea. British Library, Add. MS 5111, f. 10

New Testament, made
at Constantinople in the
middle of the 10th
century. Beginning of
the Gospel of Luke.
British Library, Add.
MS 28815, ff. 76v-77

✝ ΕΥΑΓΓΕΛΙΟΝ ΚΑΤΑ ΛΟΥΚΑΝ ·

Ἐπειδήπερ πολλοὶ ἐπεχείρησαν ἀνατάξασθαι
διήγησιν· περὶ τῶν πεπληροφορημένων
ἐν ἡμῖν πραγμάτων· καθὼς παρέδοσαν
ἡμῖν οἱ ἀπαρχῆς αὐτόπται καὶ ὑπηρέται
γενόμενοι τοῦ λόγου. Ἔδοξε κἀμοὶ παρηκολουθηκότι ἄνωθεν πᾶσιν ἀκριβῶς καθεξῆς σοι γράψαι· κράτιστε Θεόφιλε. ἵνα
ἐπιγνῷς περὶ ὧν κατηχήθης λόγων τὴν
ἀσφάλειαν· Ἐγένετο ἐν ταῖς ἡμέραις Ἡρώδου
τοῦ βασιλέως τῆς ἰουδαίας· ἱερεύς τις ὀνόματι Ζαχαρίας· ἐξ ἐφημερίας ἀβιά· καὶ ἡ
γυνὴ αὐτοῦ. ἐκ τῶν θυγατέρων ἀαρών·
καὶ τὸ ὄνομα αὐτῆς ἐλισάβετ· Ἦσαν δὲ δίκαιοι
ἀμφότεροι ἐνώπιον τοῦ θῦ· πορευό-
μενοι ἐν πάσαις ταῖς ἐντολαῖς καὶ δικαιώ-
μασιν τοῦ κῦ· ἄμεμπτοι· καὶ οὐκ ἦν αὐτοῖς
τέκνον. Καθότι ἡ ἐλισάβετ ἦν στεῖρα· καὶ
ἀμφότεροι προβεβηκότες ἐν ταῖς ἡμέραις αὐ-
τῶν ἦσαν· Ἐγένετο δὲ ἐν τῷ ἱερατεύειν
αὐτὸν ἐν τῇ τάξει τῆς ἐφημερίας αὐτοῦ·
ἔναντι τοῦ θῦ· κατὰ τὸ ἔθος τῆς ἱερατείας·

Four Gospels,
transcribed by
Constantine Pastil for
the archimandrite
Callinicus of the
Monastery of
St Demetrius the
Myroblyte in 1325/6.
Probably at the
Monastery of
St Catherine, Mount
Sinai, by the late
fifteenth century.
Beginning of the
Gospel of Luke.
British Library, Add.
MS 11838, ff. 135v-136.

ΕΥΑΝΓΕΛΙΟΝ ΚΑΤΑ ΛΟΥΚΑΝ :

Ἐπειδήπερ πολλοὶ ἐπεχείρη-
σαν· ἀνατάξασθαι διήγησιν
περὶ τῶν πεπληροφορημέ-
νων ἐν ἡμῖν πραγμάτων· καθὼς παρέδοσαν ἡμῖν οἱ ἀπ᾽
ἀρχῆς αὐτόπται καὶ ὑπηρέται
γενόμενοι τοῦ λόγου, ἔδοξε κ-
ἀμοὶ παρηκολουθηκότι ἄνωθεν
πᾶσιν ἀκριβῶς· καθεξῆς σοι γρά-
ψαι κράτιστε Θεόφιλε· ἵνα ἐπιγνῷς
περὶ ὧν κατηχήθης λόγων τὴν
ἀσφάλειαν· ἐγένετο ἐν ταῖς ἡμέραις τοῦ ἡ ᾿ρῴδου· ἐν ταῖς ἡμέραις Ἡρῴ-
δου τοῦ βασιλέως τῆς Ἰουδαίας· ἱερεύς
τις ὀνόματι Ζαχαρίας· ἐξ ἐφημερίας Ἀβιά· καὶ ἡ γυνὴ αὐτοῦ ἐκ τῶν

ΛΟСΟΥΚΟΙΔΕ
ΤΙΜΟΘΕΟΝΙ
ΑΥΤΟΥΥΜΑСΔΕ
ΕΙΡΗΚΑΦΙΛΟΥ
ΟΤΙΠΑΝΤΑΔΗ
ΚΟΥСΑΠΑΡΑΤ
ΤΡСΜΟΥΕΓΝΩ
ΡΙСΑΥΜΙΝ
ΟΥΧΥΜΕΙСΜΕ
ΕΞΕΛΕΞΑСΘΕ
ΛΛΕΓΩΕΞΕΛ
ΑΜΗΝΥΜΑС
ΚΑΘΕΘΗΚΑΥΜ
ΙΝΑΥΜΙСΥΠΑ
ΤΗΤΑΙΚΑΙΚΑΡ
ΠΟΝΦΕΡΗΤΑ

ΚΜΟΚΑΡΠΟС
ΥΜΩΝΜΕΝΕΙ
ΙΝΑΟΤΙΑΝΑΙΤΩ
СΗΤΑΙΤΟΝ
ΕΝΤΩΟΝΟΜΑ
ΤΙΜΟΥΔΩΗΥΜ
ΤΑΥΤΑΕΝΤΕΛ
ΜΑΙΥΜΙΝΙΝΑ
ΓΑΠΑΤΕΑΛΛΗΥ
ΛΟΥСΕΙΟΚΟΜ
ΜΟСΜΙСΕΙΥΜΑ
ΓΙΝΩСΚΕΤΑ
ΟΤΙΕΜΕΠΡΩ
ΥΜΩΝΜΕΜΙСΗ
СΕΝΕΙΕΚΤΟΥ
ΚΟСΜΟΥΗΤΕΘ

Greek tradition of Bible production. Instead it was the Latin translation of St Jerome, compiled in the late 4th and early 5th centuries, that maintained this tradition, as witnessed by surviving Vulgate Bibles, extending from the famous Codex Amiatinus, now in Florence, but produced in the north-east of England at the beginning of the 8th century, to the Gutenberg Bible, printed in Mainz in the middle of the 15th century. There appears also to have been no Greek equivalent of the production of Latin Bibles during the Romanesque period, and certainly no equivalent of the pocket Bibles produced in Western Europe during the 13th and 14th centuries.

Regardless of period, by far the most common book of Greek Christian scriptures was one containing only the Four Gospels. Preserving the central texts of Christianity and used for reading aloud in Christian services from as early as the second century, these books came to include not only the Gospel text but also lavish adornment. Although denounced by some of the early Church Fathers, numerous deluxe copies of the Four Gospels were produced. A select few, like the 6th-century Codex Purpureus Petropolitanus, had their text written in silver and gold on purple-painted parchment. In many the opening text of each Gospel was preceded by a full-length portrait of the relevant evangelist executed in colours and gold. Some included illustrations depicting events narrated in the Gospels. Others had their covers embellished with fine metalwork and sparkling jewels. As in the case of Codex Sinaiticus, many of these manuscripts of the Christian Gospels have been preserved for centuries in Greek monasteries and more recently in libraries such as the British Library.

Codex Purpureus Petropolitanus, made in Asia Minor or Syria in the 6th century. Gospel of John 15:15-19. British Library, Cotton MS Titus C xv, f. 5

Ceremony to celebrate the signing of the partnership agreement for the Codex Sinaiticus Project at the British Library, 9 March 2005. From left to right, Dr Ekkehard Henschke, Director of Leipzig University Library; Lynne Brindley, Chief Executive of the British Library; His Eminence Archbishop Damianos of Sinai; and Dr Alexander Bukreyev, Deputy Director of the Russian National Library, St Petersburg.

THE FUTURE FOR CODEX SINAITICUS

The British Library is currently leading an ambitious international project focused on the Codex Sinaiticus, the overall goal of which is to make the whole surviving Codex accessible to a global audience for the very first time. Using innovative digital and web-based technology and drawing on the expertise of leading scholars, conservators and curators from the UK, Europe, Russia, Egypt and the USA, the project will reunite in virtual form all four surviving parts of the Codex, now dispersed between London, Leipzig, St Petersburg and Sinai. In 2005 each of the stewards of the four distributed parts of the manuscript signed an historic partnership agreement committing them to the project which will be developed between 2006 and 2010 with the support of major benefactors and funders.

The Codex Sinaiticus Project encompasses four strands: conservation, digitisation, transcription and scholarly commentary, and dissemination of the work. Additionally, the British Library is leading research into the full history of the Codex. The results of this research will be published as part of the products of the project. Amongst these products will be a new hard-copy facsimile of the Codex and a free-to-view website, incorporating new digital images of the whole manuscript and a new scholarly transcription of the entire text, including the corrections. By this means the project aspires to continue the crucial role played by the Monastery of St Catherine, Mount Sinai, and the British Library in preserving the Greek written heritage.

PRESERVING THE GREEK
WRITTEN HERITAGE AT THE MONASTERY OF
ST CATHERINE, MOUNT SINAI

Nicholas Pickwoad

The conservation of a library of the age, importance, size and sheer complexity as that in the Monastery of Saint Catherine demands special treatment. With manuscripts dating from the 4th to the 19th centuries and an outstanding collection of printed books, to say nothing of a large collection of liturgical and diplomatic scrolls, the range of material and provenance is impressive. Equally remarkable is the preservation of so many of the bound books in their first or early bindings, which, with their complex layers of use and repair, lends the collection something of the character of an archæological site.

Interior of the Library at the Monastery of St Catherine, Mount Sinai

The remoteness and the mostly arid conditions of the Sinai desert and the determination of the fathers to preserve their books have acted to preserve the collection in a way that few other libraries could hope to. In the 21st century, however, the relative ease of travel to the monastery, growing demands from the scholarly world and the possibilities of modern conservation provide an incentive to secure the collection and protect it into the future.

It was for these reasons that, at the request of the monastery, the Saint Catherine Foundation was established in 1996 under the patronage of the Prince of Wales to raise funds to support the preservation of the library.

Work had been carried out on the manuscripts by conservators from Athens following the discovery of the New Finds in 1975, but the work of the Foundation offered the possibility of a more radical, holistic approach to the preservation of the library. This is to include the renovation of the entire top floor of the south range of the monastery which houses the library, to designs which are now being drawn up by Porphyrios Associates in London. The work will include the reshelving of all the books and scrolls and a new conservation workshop and digitising studios.

A conservation project was established at the Camberwell College of Arts (part of the University of the Arts, London) in 1996. The work done so far has included a detailed and comprehensive survey of the 3,307 bound manuscripts in the Old Library (completed on 4 March 2006), the design of a new stainless-steel box to protect each of the 2000 more important and fragile bound manuscripts, detailed reports on some of the most important manuscripts in need of conservation (including the leaves of Codex Sinaiticus), the removal of early manuscript leaves from the walls of one of the cells ahead of building repairs and the preparation of books and documents for display both in the monastery's own museum and for loan abroad. The data from the survey is currently being incorporated into a database, which will also contain digitised copies of the approximately 30,000 slides taken during the survey. This work is being supported by a grant from the Arts and Humanities Research Council of Great Britain and will also result in an Anglo-Greek bookbinding terminology. When completed, the database will be used to draw up the programmes of conservation work which will start in the conservation workshop as soon as it is completed.

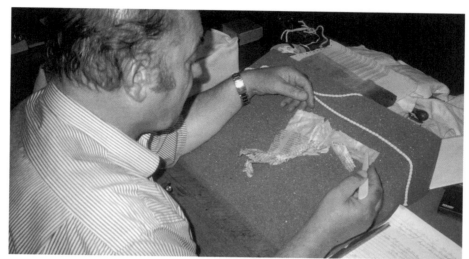

Christopher Clarkson assessing part of Codex Sinaiticus at the Monastery of St Catherine, Mount Sinai, in September 2003

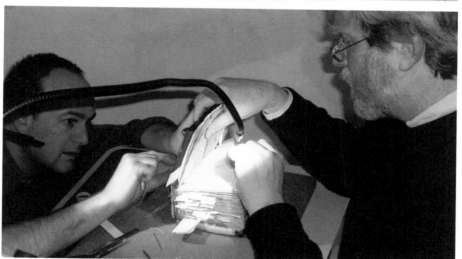

Nicholas Pickwoad and Andrew Honey conserving MS gr. 418 at the Monastery of St Catherine, Mount Sinai, in February 2006

FURTHER READING

CODEX SINAITICUS *Codex Friderico-Augustanus*. Ed. Constantine Tischendorf. Leipzig, 1846. • *Bibliorum Codex Sinaiticus Petropolitanus*. Ed. Constantine Tischendorf. 4 vols. St Petersburg, 1862. • F. H. A. Scrivener. *A Full Collation of the Codex Sinaiticus with the Received Text of the New Testament.* Cambridge: Deighton Bell, 1864; 2nd edn 1867. • .*When were our Gospels written? An Argument by Constantine Tischendorf with a Narrative of the Discovery of the Sinaitic Manuscript.* London: Religious Tract Society, 1866. • .Constantine Tischendorf. *The New Testament: The Authorised English Version; With Introduction, and Various Readings from the Three Most Celebrated Manuscripts of the Original Greek Text.* Leipzig: Bernhard Tauchnitz, 1869. • .Kirsopp and Helen Lake. *Codex Sinaiticus Petropolitanus.* 2 vols. Oxford: University Press, 1911, 1922.• .Harry Tompkins Anderson. *The New Testament, translated from the Sinaitic Manuscript discovered by Constantine Tischendorf at Mount Sinai.* Cincinnati: The Standard Publishing Company, 1918. • .H. J. M. Milne and T. C. Skeat. *Scribes and Correctors of the Codex Sinaiticus.* London: The British Museum, 1938. • *Codex Sinaiticus and Codex Alexandrinus.* 2nd edn. London: The British Museum, 1951. • .Gordon P. Fee. 'Codex Sinaiticus in the Gospel of John: A Contribution to Methodology in Establishing Textual Relationships'. *New Testament Studies,* 15 (1968-69), pp. 23-44. • .T. S. Pattie. 'The Codex Sinaiticus'. *The British Library Journal,* 3 (1977), pp. 1-6. • .Ihor Sevčenko. 'New Documents on Constantine Tischendorf and the Codex Sinaiticus'. *Scriptorium,* 34 (1980), pp. 55-80. • .James Bentley. *Secrets of Mount Sinai. The Story of the World's Oldest Bible – Codex Sinaiticus.* London: Orbis, 1985. • .T. S. Pattie. 'The Creation of the Great Codices'. *The Bible as Book. The Manuscript Tradition.* Ed. John L. Sharpe III and Kimberly Van Kampen. London: The British Library, 1998, pp. 61-72. • .T. C. Skeat. 'The "Codex Sinaiticus", the "Codex Vaticanus" and Constantine'. *Journal of Theological Studies,* 50 (1999), pp. 583-625. • .John J. Brogan. 'Another Look at Codex Sinaiticus'. *The Bible as Book. The Transmission of the Greek Text.* Ed. Scot McKendrick and Orlaith O'Sullivan. London: The British Library, 2003, pp. 17-32. • .A. V. Zakharova. 'Obzor materialov rossijskih arhivov o priobretenii Sinajskoj Biblij'. *Vtorye chtenija pamiati professora N. F. Kaptereva (Moskva, 28-29 oktiabria 2004). Materialy.* Moscow, 2004, pp. 33-45 • .Dirk Jongkind. 'Studies in Scribal Habits of Codex Sinaiticus'. D.Phil. thesis, Cambridge University, 2005. • .Amy Catherine Myshrall. 'Codex Sinaiticus, its Correctors, and the Caesarean Text of the Gospels'. Ph.D. thesis, Birmingham University, 2005. • .GREEK MANUSCRIPTS OF THE BIBLE Jack Finegan. *Encountering New Testament Manuscripts: A Working Introduction to Textual Criticism.* London: S.P.C.K., 1975. • .Bruce M. Metzger. *Manuscripts of the Bible. An Introduction to Greek Palaeography.* 2nd edn. New York: Oxford University Press, 1991. • .K. Aland. *Kurzgefasste Liste der Griechischen Handschriften des Neuen Testaments.* 2nd edn. New York: De Gruyter, 1994. • .T. S. Pattie. *Manuscripts of the Bible: Greek Bibles in the British Library.* 2nd edn. London: The British Library, 1995.

First published 2006 by The British Library 96 Euston Road London NW1 2DB

© 2006 The British Library Board

ISBN 0 7123 4940 5

A CIP record for this book is available from the British Library

Designed and typeset in Monotype Dante by et al–design. Printed in England at the University Press, Cambridge